Best Hikes Near
Nashville

Best Hikes Near
Nashville

KEITH STELTER

FALCONGUIDES

GUILFORD, CONNECTICUT
HELENA, MONTANA

AN IMPRINT OF GLOBE PEQUOT PRESS

FALCONGUIDES®

FalconGuides is an imprint of Globe Pequot Press.
Falcon, FalconGuides, and Outfit Your Mind are registered trademarks of Morris Book Publishing, LLC.

Interior photos by Keith Stelter
Text design: Sheryl P. Kober
Maps: Mapping Specialists © Morris Book Publishing LLC
Project editor: Julie Marsh
Layout artist: Melissa Evarts

Library of Congress Cataloging-in-Publication Data

Stelter, Keith.
  Best hikes near Nashville / Keith Stelter.
    p. cm. — (FalconGuides)
  ISBN 978-0-7627-5980-4
  1. Hiking—Tennessee—Nashville Region—Guidebooks. 2. Trails—Tennessee—
Nashville Region—Guidebooks. 3. Nashville Region (Tenn.)—Guidebooks. I. Title.
  GV199.42.T22N378 2011
  917.68'5504—dc22
                        2010042880

Printed in the United States of America

10 9 8 7 6 5 4 3 2 1

Contents

Overview

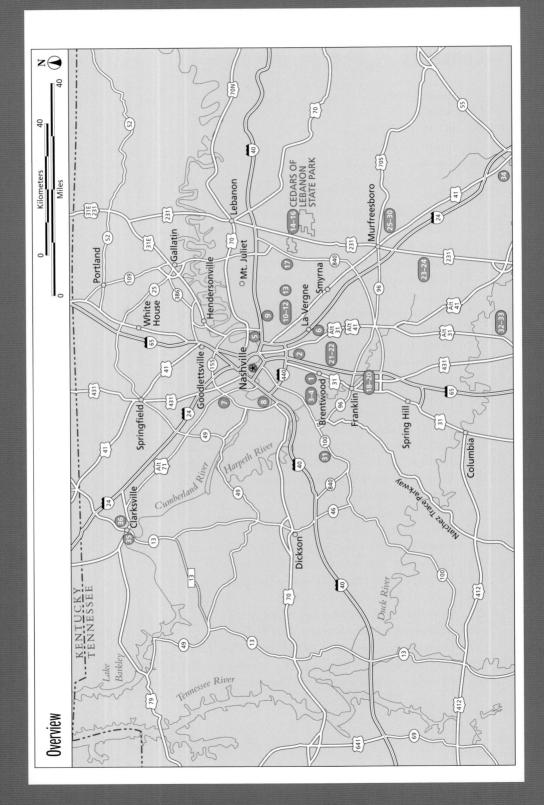

Ducks float down the Little Harpeth River.

Acknowledgments

Many people helped make this book possible, and a few went "beyond the call of duty." Thanks to Mark, Scott, and Kay Stelter for their encouragement, ideas, patience, and proofreading; Nate Enloe for his general help; and Kevin Stelter, Olivia and Justin Stelter, and Shae Simpkins with Madison for hiking and journaling with me. Special thanks to Kay and Rod Heller for their southern hospitality in allowing me to use their guesthouse as my base while in Nashville. Thanks to Thurman Mullins, park superintendent at Long Hunter State Park. Dozens of other people provided information about history, geology, flora, fauna, karst areas, and hikes they consider the "best hikes near Nashville." I appreciate their work and thank all of them.

An American Beauty butterfly sips nectar from a thistle bloom.

Introduction

The purpose of this guide is to introduce readers to the variety of hiking opportunities in the Nashville area, including Antioch, Burns, Clarksville, Franklin, Brentwood, Hermitage, Murfreesboro, and Lebanon. In many hiking guides the hike descriptions are generally point-to-point narratives, getting you safely from the trailhead to the trail's end and back again. However, including information on area flora, fauna, history, and geology adds a great deal of interest to many hikers, including families with young children.

I spent several months researching, talking with park personnel and other folks, hiking and sometimes re-hiking trails, and studying the area for interesting facts, scenery, history, geology, and potential photographs. I talked with a variety of hikers, asking them what they wanted a hike description to cover and what made a "best hike near Nashville." I used the following criteria to select the hikes included in this guide: fun, exercise, family experience, scenery, history, first-time hiker, experienced hiker, moderate length (1 to 5 miles), dog friendliness, and wheelchair and stroller accessibility. Loops and interconnecting loop trails were selected where possible so that a "best" hike within a park could be fashioned by combining the best of several trails.

The Little Falls of the Duck River is located along the Mounds Trail (hike 34).

Determining the best hikes near Nashville was a combination of personal judgment about what level of hiker the hike was geared to and information from park staff and other hikers. Four of my favorite hikes are the varied trails at Long Hunter State Park, the interconnecting loops in Cedars of Lebanon, the Old Stone Fort trails, and the Barfield Crescent Park trails. Hiking city and county trails offers a different experience from hiking in state parks and on backcountry trails. Most of the city trails are multipurpose and paved; a few are lighted at night, creating an entirely new hiking experience. There also can be the distraction of the city itself, with its busy streets, buildings, and commerce, but surprisingly many of the trails are in wooded areas, providing an unexpected degree of solitude.

Whether providing recreational or educational opportunities, encouraging well-being, exploring history or geology, or bringing together people of all ages, hiking has become an important part of many people's lives. The photographs were chosen to whet your curiosity about a hike. The "In Addition" sidebars and stories are meant to be enjoyable, informative, and educational, helping to make this a family book. I hope that at least some of the hikes in this guide will become your personal favorites and that this book will prove an informative and interesting read as well as an excellent guide to the best hikes near Nashville.

Hiking around Nashville is more than walking along rivers. Trails can be found in woods, forests, nature sanctuaries, downtown, or along an Army Corps

Geese sun themselves along a Bowie Woods trail (hike 31).

of Engineers lake. Some trails are busy with hikers, joggers, and cyclists; others are secluded and far from downtown.

A dimension can be added to any hike by watching for birds, trying to identify them, and enjoying their songs. The best indication of birds being present is hearing their songs. The bluebird sings *chur-lee chur chur-lee,* the eastern phoebe repeats *fee-bee fee-bee* from the tops of branches, and the tufted titmouse makes a loud, whistle-like *peter peter peter.* Some of the area's most colorful birds include the red-breasted nuthatch, eastern bluebird, yellow-throated warbler, dickcissel, pileated woodpecker, American goldfinch, vermilion flycatcher, and numerous ducks, such as the hooded merganser.

Most mammals are active during the night, so seeing them can be difficult. Look for their tracks around the trail, near streams, and at the edge of woods. White-tailed deer, coyotes, opossums, foxes, raccoons, skunks, and fox squirrels make their homes here. Squirrels, white-tailed deer, and raccoons are especially common in many hiking areas.

In the spring and early summer, when wildflowers set the roadsides ablaze with color, driving to a hiking location can be a visual feast. The passion flower is the state wildflower, and its white flowers bloom from summer through autumn.

Nashville is the capital and second-largest city in Tennessee. An advantage to hikers is that much of the city was built on forested land and along rivers. Some of these areas have been set aside as parks, with miles of trails. The trails (greenways) along the rivers are called "linear" because they follow the river and are generally out-and-back hikes.

The Nashville Parks & Recreation Department's trail system spans more than 60 miles. Enjoy the experience of hiking in middle Tennessee. The great ecological diversity of the territory, along with the flora, fauna, and karst geology, allows you to fashion trips that are much more than just "hikes in the woods." City hiking trails are sometimes sidewalks, and some have been widened from the conventional 4-foot sidewalk to as much as 13 feet to allow multiuse. Some of these sidewalks have been designed as "traffic lanes" (still called trails) to accommodate persons walking and biking to work as well as recreationists.

Nashville's Weather

Nashville's climate is humid and subtropical, with hot summers and cool winters. The area can experience snowfall, but it usually is gone the next morning. March signals the start of spring, with warmer weather and colorful displays of flowering trees and shrubs. From March to mid-May, temperatures average between 45 and 70 degrees Fahrenheit. Summer brings warmer weather accompanied by high humidity. The average relative humidity in Nashville is 83 percent in the mornings and 60 percent in the afternoons. Mid to late October has cooler temperatures, encouraging brilliant fall colors.

The lowest average temperature (37 degrees) is in January, and the highest average (80 degrees) is in July. The average yearly rainfall is 48.1 inches. The wettest month is May, averaging 5 inches, and the driest month is October, with 2.9 inches of rain.

Current weather and forecasts for the Nashville area can be obtained by calling the park contact for the hike you are considering. Except for high temperatures in July and August and possible showers in May, the weather for hiking in the area is generally great year-round.

Enjoy luxurious fauna three seasons of the year in Nashville (hike 32).

Average Monthly Temperatures

Month	High	Low
January	46	28
February	52	31
March	61	39
April	70	47
May	77	57
June	85	65
July	89	70
August	88	68
September	82	61
October	71	49
November	59	40
December	49	32

Average Precipitation (Rainfall)

Month	Inches
January	3.9
February	3.7
March	4.9
April	3.9
May	5.0
June	4.0
July	3.8
August	3.3
September	3.6
October	2.9
November	4.4
December	4.5

Leave No Trace and Trail Etiquette

We have a responsibility to protect, no longer just conquer and use, our wild places. Many public hiking locations are at risk, so please do what you can to use them wisely. The following list will help you better understand what it means to take care of parks and wild places while still making the most of your hiking experience.

- Stay on the trail. Anyone can take a hike, but hiking safely and with good conservation practices is an art requiring preparation and proper equipment. Always leave an area as good as—or preferably better—than you found it. The key to doing this is staying on the trail.

It's true that a trail anywhere leads nowhere new, but purists will just have to get over it. Trails serve an important purpose: They limit impact on natural areas. Straying from a designated trail can cause damage to sensitive areas— damage that may take the area years to recover from, if it can recover at all. Even simple shortcuts can be destructive.

Many of the hikes described in this guide are on or near areas ecologically important to supporting endangered flora and fauna. So, please, stay on the trail.

- Leave no weeds. Noxious weeds tend to overtake other plants, which in turn affects animals and birds that depend on native plants for food. To minimize the spread of noxious weeds, regularly clean your boots and hiking poles of mud and seeds and brush your dog to remove any weed seeds before heading into a new area. Nonnative invasive plants such as Cheat

These butterflies won't bother you (hike 15).

Grass and and Chinese Privet are particularly destructive and can quickly destroy acres of habitat.

- Keep your dog under control. Always obey leash laws, and be sure to bury your dog's waste or pack it out in plastic bags.
- Respect other trail users. Often you won't be the only one on the trail. With the rise in popularity of multiuse trails, you'll have to learn a new kind of respect, beyond the nod and "hello" approach of the past. First investigate whether you're on a multiuse trail, and then assume the appropriate precautions. Mountain bikers can be like stealth airplanes—you may not hear them coming. Be prepared and find out ahead of time whether you share the trail with them. Cyclists should always yield to hikers, but that's little comfort to the hiker who gets overrun. Be aware, and stay to the right. More trails are being designed to be, at least in part, wheelchair accessible. Always step to the side to allow folks in wheelchairs time to navigate the terrain, and make them aware if you are going to pass around them.

Precautions and First Aid

Sunburn

Wear sunscreen or sunblock, protective clothing, and a wide-brimmed hat. If you do get sunburn, protect the affected area from further sun exposure and treat it

A trough is cut from native lumber (hike 34).

with aloe vera gel or a treatment of your choice. Remember that your eyes are vulnerable to damaging radiation as well. Sunglasses can help prevent eye damage from the sun.

Blisters

Be prepared to take care of these hike spoilers by carrying moleskin (a lightly padded adhesive) or gauze and tape. An effective way to apply moleskin is to cut out a circle of the material, remove the center—like a doughnut—and place it over the blistered area.

Insect Bites and Stings

You can treat most insect bites and stings by taking an anti-inflammatory pain medication and using ice to reduce swelling. A cold compress can sometimes ease the itching and discomfort. Don't pinch or scratch the area—you'll only spread the venom.

Ticks

Ticks can carry diseases such as Rocky Mountain spotted fever and Lyme disease. The best defense is, of course, prevention. If you know you're going to be hiking through an area containing ticks, wear long pants and a long-sleeved shirt. At the end of your hike, do a spot check for ticks (and insects in general).

The end of a perfect day (hike 7).

Poison Ivy, Oak, and Sumac

These skin irritants are prevalent on many of the trails in the Nashville area, sometimes growing into the trail. They come in the form of a bush or a vine and have leaflets in groups of three (poison ivy and oak), five, seven, or nine. Learn how to spot the plants, and especially show young children what to look for. Few things can spoil a hike, or your life the week after, than coming into contact with poison ivy, oak, or sumac. The allergic reaction, in the form of blisters, usually develops about twelve hours after exposure.

The best defense against these irritants is to wear clothing that covers your arms, legs, and torso. If you think you came in contact with these plants, wash the affected area with soap and water as soon as possible. If the rash spreads, you may need to see a doctor.

Wildflowers decorate the trails (hike 9).

How to Use This Guide

Thirty-six hikes are detailed in this guide. The overview map at the beginning of the book shows the location of each hike by hike number, keyed to the table of contents. Each hike is accompanied by a route map that shows access roads, the highlighted featured route, and arrows to point you in the right direction. It indicates the general outline of the hike, but due to scale restrictions, it is not as detailed as a park map might be or even as our "Miles and Directions" are. While most of the hikes are on clearly designated paths, use these route maps in conjunction with other resources.

To aid in decision-making, each hike description begins with a short summary to give you a taste of the hiking adventure to follow. You'll learn about the trail terrain and what surprises the route has to offer. Next you'll find the quick, nitty-gritty details of the hike: hike distance and type (loop, lollipop, or out and back); approximate hiking time; difficulty rating; type of trail surface; best season for the hike; other trail users; canine compatibility; fees and permits; park schedule; map resources; trail contacts; and additional information that will help you on your trek.

Finding the trailhead provides directions from Nashville right down to where you'll want to park your car. **The Hike** is the meat of the chapter. Detailed and honest, it's a carefully researched impression of the trail. While it's impossible to cover everything, you can rest assured that you won't miss what's important. **Miles and Directions** provides mileage cues that identify all turns and trail name changes, as well as points of interest.

Don't feel restricted to the routes and trails mapped in this guide. Stick to marked trails, but be adventurous and use the book as a platform to discover new routes for yourself. One of the simplest ways to begin is to turn the map upside down and hike the trail in reverse. The change in perspective can make the hike feel quite different; it's like getting two hikes for one. You may wish to copy the route directions onto a sheet of paper to help you while hiking, or photocopy the map and cue sheet to take with you. Otherwise, just slip the whole book in your pocket and bring it along.

Enjoy your time in the outdoors—and remember to pack out what you pack in.

Trail Finder

Hike No.	Hike Name	Best Hikes for Families and Children	Best Hikes for Lake, River, and Stream Lovers	Best Hikes for History Lovers	Best Hikes for Nature Lovers and Bird Watchers	Best Hikes for Dogs	Best Hikes for the Physically Challenged	Best Hikes for Geology Fans	Best Hikes for Cedar Glade Lovers	Best Hikes for Sun Lovers	Best Hikes for Forest Lovers
1	Radnor Lake State Natural Area: Spillway Trail and Lake Trail	●	●								●
2	Ellington Agricultural Center: Eagle Trail and Roberts Walk	●	●		●						
3	Edwin Warner Park: Geology Trail		●			●		●			●
4	Edwin Warner Park: Scenic Road Trail										●
5	Stones River Greenway: McGavock Spring House Trail		●		●						
6	Mill Creek Greenway Trail	●	●								
7	Beaman Park: Creekside Trail and Henry Hollow Loop		●		●	●					●
8	Bells Bend: Poplar Hollow Trail				●						
9	Percy Priest Lake: Three Hickories Trail	●	●								●
10	Long Hunter State Park: Couchville Lake Trail	●	●				●			●	●
11	Long Hunter State Park: Deer Trail	●	●								
12	Long Hunter State Park: Jones Mill Mountain Bike Trail				●						●

Trail Finder

Hike No.	Hike Name	Best Hikes for Families and Children	Best Hikes for Lake, River, and Stream Lovers	Best Hikes for History Lovers	Best Hikes for Nature Lovers and Bird Watchers	Best Hikes for Dogs	Best Hikes for the Physically Challenged	Best Hikes for Geology Fans	Best Hikes for Cedar Glade Lovers	Best Hikes for Sun Lovers	Best Hikes for Forest Lovers
13	Couchville Cedar Glade State Natural Area: Tyler Alley Sykes Trail										
14	Cedars of Lebanon State Park: Cedar Woods Trail							●	●	●	●
15	Cedars of Lebanon State Park: Cedar Glade Interpretive Trail	●							●		
16	Cedars of Lebanon State Park: Limestone Sink Trail	●						●			
17	Vesta Cedar Glade State Natural Area								●		
18	East Flank—Battle of Franklin	●	●	●							
19	Pinkerton Park: Fort Granger Trail	●	●	●							
20	Franklin Greenway: Aspen Grove Trail	●	●		●						
21	Brentwood Greenway: River Park Trail	●	●				●				
22	Brentwood Greenway: Crockett Park Trail	●	●			●	●				
23	Barfield Crescent Park: Wilderness Traill							●	●		●
24	Barfield Crescent Park: Rocky Trail							●			●

Trail Finder

Hike No.	Hike Name	Best Hikes for Families and Children	Best Hikes for Lake, River, and Stream Lovers	Best Hikes for History Lovers	Best Hikes for Nature Lovers and Bird Watchers	Best Hikes for Dogs	Best Hikes for the Physically Challenged	Best Hikes for Geology Fans	Best Hikes for Cedar Glade Lovers	Best Hikes for Sun Lovers	Best Hikes for Forest Lovers
25	Murfreesboro Greenway: Cason Trail		●				●				
26	Murfreesboro Greenway: Manson Pike Trail	●	●		●	●					
27	Murfreesboro Greenway: College Street Pond Loop	●			●	●	●				
28	Stones River National Battlefield: Cotton Field Trail & Boundary Trail			●							
29	Stones River Greenway: Fortress Rosecrans Loop	●	●	●							
30	Murfreesboro Greenway: Thompson Lane to Broad Street		●	●						●	
31	Bowie Woods: Bowie Lakes Loop		●			●					
32	Henry Horton State Park: Hickory Ridge Nature Loop	●			●			●			●
33	Henry Horton State Park: Wilhoite Mill Loop and Fisherman Trail		●	●							●
34	Old Stone Fort State Archaeological Park: Mounds Loop		●	●			●				●
35	Clarksville Greenway: Zone C	●				●					
36	Dunbar Cave State Natural Area: Lake Trail and Recovery Trail		●	●							●

Map Legend

Transportation

40	Freeway/Interstate Highway
431	U.S. Highway
96	State Highway
1431	Other Road
= = = =	Unpaved Road
+—+—+	Railroad

Trails

-------	Featured Route
- - - - -	Trail or Fire Road
———	Paved Trail
→	Direction of Travel
‖‖‖‖‖‖‖	Boardwalk/Steps

Water Features

	Body of Water
	River or Creek
	Marsh

Symbols

▭	Bench
⏝	Bridge
■	Building/Point of Interest
▲	Campground
★	Capital
∩	Cave
P	Parking
×	Physical Feature
🎪	Picnic Area
🚻	Restroom
◄	Scenic View
☎	Telephone
○	Towns and Cities
20	Trailhead
?	Visitor/Information Center
🚰	Water

Land Management

▭	Local & State Parks/Forest
⸽ ⸽	Natural Area

Radnor Lake State Natural Area: Spillway Trail and Lake Trail

This hike takes you around the lake and through heavy woods containing beech, tulip poplar, and sugar maple. April and May offer bird-watchers the best opportunity to see many of the 238 species that frequent the woods and lake. An observation deck and several well-placed benches furnish resting places to kick back and enjoy nature.

Start: Spillway Trail trailhead behind visitor center

Distance: 3.5-mile clockwise loop

Approximate hiking time: 3 hours

Difficulty: Moderate due to some steep slopes

Trail surface: Dirt, rock

Best season: Year-round

Other trail users: Bird-watchers

Canine compatibility: Dogs not permitted

Fees and permits: None required

Schedule: 6:00 a.m. to dark

Maps: USGS: Oak Hill; trail maps available at visitor center

Trail contact: Manager, Radnor Lake State Natural Area, 1160 Otter Creek Rd., Nashville, TN 37220; (615) 373-3467; www.radnorlake.org

Other: Restrooms and water are available at the visitor center; no potable water or restrooms on the trail. Take adequate drinking water, and use sunscreen and insect repellant. Several sections of the trail have sharp drop-offs, so keep young children in hand. Joggers and cyclists are prohibited on trails.

Finding the trailhead: From I-65 South in downtown Nashville, exit at Harding Place and go west. Harding Place turns into Battery Lane. Turn left on Granny White Pike and go about 2 miles, then turn left (east) on Otter Creek Road to 1160 Otter Creek Rd. and the visitor center and parking area. *DeLorme Tennessee Atlas & Gazetteer:* Page 53, D5. GPS: N36 03.80' / W86 48.61'

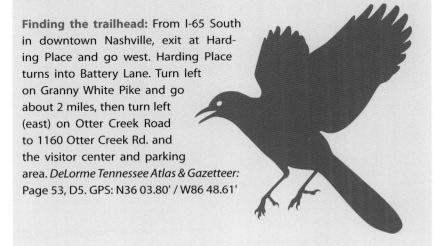

Before your hike, stop at the visitor center to pick up a trail map. Follow the boardwalk at the rear of the visitor center to the Spillway Trail; the trailhead is on the left. This trail heads east and connects to the Lake Trail.

Soon you'll reach an observation deck—take a moment to look for animals and birds. The lake is not in view, but a small unnamed creek flows past the deck. The lake and the park's 1,200 acres are a state natural area and a magnet for water-birds. It serves as a winter sanctuary for many species of ducks, including gadwall, American widgeon, canvasback, and bufflehead.

Take a hard left after the observation deck and then a quick right, passing a two-rail fence on the right. Reach the spillway bridge on the right and take a short out and back to the spillway. Butterflies like to congregate in this area. The bridge also furnishes one of the better views of the lake and affords excellent photo ops. Return to the trail as the Spillway Trail turns into the Lake Trail.

Good canopy cover furnishes shade on this section of the hike. At bench 13 make a hard left, heading down to an overlook deck with two benches at the edge of the lake. Look to the right and left to see various vines, including poison ivy, climbing on large oak and hickory trees. The lake, which is on the right, is hidden by trees and undergrowth.

A group of park volunteers resurface a trail at Radnor Lake SNA.

After passing bench 21, cross a wood bridge across a swampy section. Look for white-tailed deer in this area in the early morning or late afternoon. Follow the trail as it weaves to the right and left and back again and goes up and down slopes. Listen and look for signs of woodpeckers, especially the yellow-bellied sapsucker. It is medium size, about 8 to 9 inches long, with a red forehead patch. Look for sugar maple trees with rows of small, round holes girdling their trunks, where sapsuckers have searched for sap and insects.

The woods are still predominantly oak and hickory, but beeches and tulip poplars may also be seen. In the spring look for mountain laurel and elderberries, which are not commonly found in this central basin area. Continue following the trail generally south until reaching a T. Take the right branch, still heading south toward the lake. The left branch leads to the 1.5-mile Ganier Ridge Trail. Keep an eye out for rat snakes and king snakes. These non-venomous snakes are fairly common in the park.

Near the southeast corner of the lake, cross a bridge and bear right. In the spring look for wildflowers, mosses, and ferns growing along the edge of the trail. Continue generally south until reaching a Y, and take the right branch to stay on the Lake Trail. Listen for birds singing in the woods, including crested flycatchers and scarlet tanagers. Add an extra dimension to the hike by carrying a bird guidebook to help identify some of the more than 200 species found in the park.

Continue following the trail south, then bear west and cross a bridge over a swampy area that has bench 29 at its center. This is a good spot to rest before getting to the ridges of the South Lake Trail. Almost immediately follow along a causeway heading west and intersecting Otter Creek Road (the park road), and turn right onto the asphalt road. The lake is in view to the right about 5 feet away. The area between the road and water is a favorite spot for water snakes, including the venomous water moccasin. Turtles and waterbirds, including ducks, are often seen here.

Cross Otter Creek Road to reach the connector trail to the South Lake Trail. Thirty-seven steps lead up to this narrow trail that wiggles and squiggles through the woods and up the ridge. Use caution because the right edge of the trail drops off sharply down to the road. At bench 51 bear left, heading generally northwest, and cross a bridge. Reach a Y and take the right branch, continuing on the South Lake Trail. This is one of the most strenuous sections of the hike.

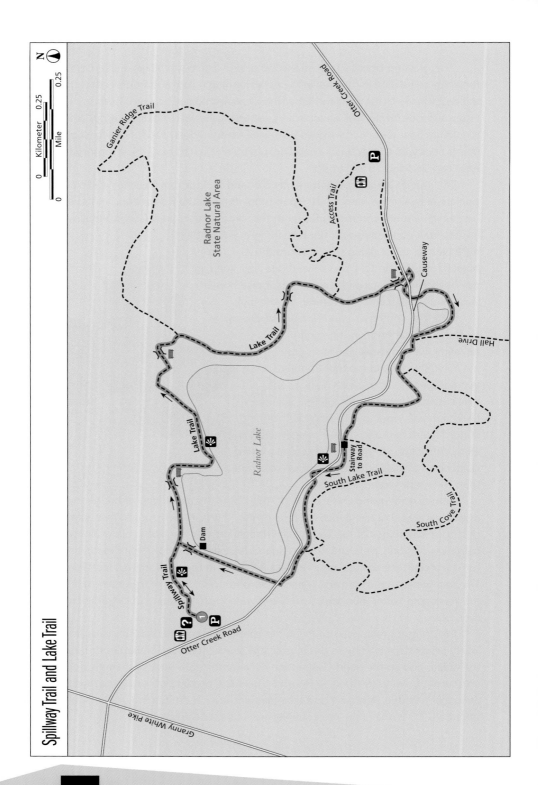

Spillway Trail and Lake Trail

Ganier Ridge Trail

Radnor Lake
State Natural Area

Otter Creek Road

Access Trail

Causeway

Hall Drive

Lake Trail

Lake Trail

Radnor Lake

Stairway
to Road

South Lake Trail

South Cove Trail

Dam

Spillway Trail

Otter Creek Road

Granny White Pike

N

Kilometer   0.25
0   0.25
0
Mile

Reach an intersection on the right that has sixteen steps leading down. Go down the steps and cross a bridge; to the right is a view of Radnor Lake. Cross another short bridge and immediately bear left, still going generally northwest. Try to identify the various hardwood trees in the woods around the trail.

You then reach more steps on the right, going down to Otter Creek Road. Go down the steps and turn left, heading northwest onto Otter Creek Road. Follow the road northwest to the Dam Walkway. Cross the walkway and stop to view the lake. Follow the walkway northeast and cross the spillway bridge, which connects with the Spillway Trail. Turn left, heading west onto the Spillway Trail, and backtrack to the visitor center.

MILES AND DIRECTIONS

0.0 Start at the back of the visitor center and follow the boardwalk to the Spillway Trail trailhead.

0.1 Within 0.1 mile reach a T and take the left branch onto the Lake Trail. Head south, then north, and then east as the loop trail heads clockwise around Radnor Lake. Reach an observation deck on the right and pass bench 6.

0.2 Pass bench 8 on the left and the spillway and spillway bridge on the right.

0.4 Pass bench 10 on the left; Radnor Lake is about 30 feet away. Continue on the trail and reach a wood bridge. After crossing the bridge, make a hard right. Pass bench 12 on the left.

0.5 Bear left up a slight slope and reach bench 13 on the right. Take a hard left toward the lake and an overlook deck with benches 14 and 15. Bear right around the lake.

0.8 Continue following the trail generally east. Pass benches 18, 19, and 20.

0.9 Bear slightly left and pass bench 21. Reach a wood bridge and cross it. Bear hard right at the end of the bridge and go up a slight slope while following to the left and then right.

1.1 Reach a T and take the right branch. The left branch leads to the Ganier Ridge Trail. Follow the trail as it slopes up and down. Pass benches 22, 23, and 24. Bear left from bench 24.

1.3 Bear sweeping left and then hard left away from the lake. The lake cannot be seen.

1.5 Bear slightly to the right and reach a wood bridge over a dry creek bed. Follow the trail, bearing slightly right, and almost immediately reach a Y. Take the right branch, following the Lake Trail, and pass bench 25.

1.6 Reach a Y and take the right branch, following the Lake Trail. The left branch leads to the Ganier Ridge Trail. Continue following the trail, bearing slightly left and up, and pass bench 28. Radnor Lake can be seen through the trees to the right, about 200 feet away.

1.8 Reach a wood bridge over a swampy area. Bench 29 is at the middle of the bridge. Cross the bridge and pass bench 30. Almost immediately reach Otter Creek Road; follow the road to the right. Radnor Lake is to the right about 5 feet away and 5 feet down. There is water on the right and left. Follow the road along the edge of Radnor Lake.

2.0 Pass a road to the left that leads to the Environmental Education Center. Continue following Otter Creek Road.

2.1 Carefully cross Otter Creek Road to the trailhead and steps leading up the hill to the South Cove Trail and South Lake Trail. Climb the thirty-seven steps and follow the South Lake Trail as it heads south, then north, and then west in the woods above Otter Creek Road. At bench 51 bear left and immediately reach a short wood bridge. Cross the bridge and continue on the South Lake Trail.

2.2 Reach a Y and take the right branch, continuing on the South Lake Trail. This section is one of the most strenuous parts of the trail. Continue following the trail, bearing hard right and then up a moderately steep slope.

2.3 Come to sixteen steps. Go down the steps and reach a wood bridge about 18 feet long. Cross the bridge and follow the trail as it slopes down. Pass bench 50 as the trail continues to head slightly down.

Albert Ganier, the founder of the Tennessee Ornithological Society, was instrumental in persuading the Louisville & Nashville Railroad to declare Radnor Lake a wildlife sanctuary in 1923.

2.4 Continue following the trail generally northwest and cross a short bridge. Radnor Lake can be seen on the right across Otter Creek Road, which is about 40 feet down the hill. Immediately after the bridge, bear left and then right, going slightly uphill. Pass a path on the right that leads down to the road.

2.6 Reach steps on the right leading down to the road. Go down the thirty-six steps and turn left onto Otter Creek Road. Radnor Lake is to the right of the road.

2.7 Pass an observation deck that overlooks the lake and has two benches. Continue following the road, bearing slightly to the left.

2.9 Pass a Y on the left that is a connector for the South Cove Trail and South Lake Trail. Continue on the road.

3.0 Look to the right for the trail across the dam spillway. Cross the road and follow the trail across the spillway. At the end of the spillway, reach a T and take the left branch. Backtrack to the trailhead and visitor center.

3.5 End the hike at the trailhead and visitor center.

Sam Houston (1793–1863), a native of Tennessee, served as governor of Tennessee from 1828 to 1829. He then moved to Texas and became that state's governor (1858 to 1861).

Journaling—More Fun on the Trail

If you're not hiking with some specific purpose other than to simply enjoy the outdoors, journaling can be a great way to add a new dimension to a family or social hike. A friend of mine had recently given me some instructions on trail observation and how to keep a trail journal. Prior to that I wasn't sure what journaling was. Like the words *yodeling* and *pedaling,* it sounded interesting and as though it involved action, but I didn't know exactly what it involved or how it fit in with hiking.

My friend explained that journaling is simply keeping a rough set of notes on what you observe on or near the trail. You don't need to be a writer or scientist. The most interesting aspect is the methods of observation. These include closing your eyes and listening, scooping up some dirt to feel, and covering your ears and watching. The idea is to use all of your senses to enhance the experience.

The minimum items needed to start a journal are something to write with and something to write on. Some general guidelines on how to start the journal: In the upper right-hand corner of the page record the date, time, location, weather, and habitat for each hike. This gives a reference point for future use of the notes. Each hiker records the things that are of interest to him or her, including drawings. Some folks, like me, have difficulty drawing a stick man, but give it a try—maybe start out with a dandelion.

I decided to try out some of the techniques, which sounded like a great inexpensive family activity. I asked my son Kevin, his daughter Shae, and her seven-year-old daughter Madison to accompany me. Kevin wasn't sure what I was trying to accomplish. I convinced him that hiking and journaling would give him a chance to slow down and focus on something other than work. Madison led the way to the trail. A five-minute limit was set to walk about 75 yards up the trail at a normal pace, and fifteen minutes to return while using our new observation skills. At the end of the 75-yard walk and to our amazement, there wasn't much difference in any of the journals. All of us had seen trees, bushes, and sky. Madison had seen a couple of worms and a low-flying bee, while Kevin noticed a salamander that Shae and I had not recorded.

It was now time to start back and make more observations. We stopped every 10 to 15 yards to listen, watch, touch, smell, and possibly taste. Madison was the only one to actually taste something, taking some blooms from a honeysuckle bush and showing us they were edible. At each stop we looked straight ahead and then stooped, stood up, covered our eyes, and listened, and then covered our ears and watched. What we saw and heard became entries in our journals and included wind rustling, birds chirping, people, the path, ants, a squirrel climbing a tree, sky with clouds, pine needles and cones, small and large bushes, red flowers, poison ivy, a hole in a tree, a turkey vulture circling in the sky, and pine and hardwood trees.

Things had been felt that were hard, soft, slippery, waxy, coarse, smooth, dry, and wet. Colors noted were green, yellow, brown, black, and white and a rainbow-colored leaf. After discovering something new, we were often surprised at how many times we continued to see it and realized that we must have walked past it many times before without noticing it. The return trip almost became a game. The writing stopped being a task and became a fun part of our trip.

Back home, we were all excited about the hike. From our enthusiasm, there was no doubt that journaling had enhanced our enjoyment of the trip. Try it—you could like it!

Flower lovers will want to spend time in the Bicentennial Iris Garden that greets them at the end of the Eagle Trail. Circle a ten-acre meadow, whose eastern portion borders Seven Mile Creek, which is a year-round haven for birds. After leaving the meadow and entering heavy woods, notice some of the very large trees, including black walnut, hackberry, and sugar maple. The center is listed as an Official Arboretum by the Nashville Tree Foundation.

Start: Eagle Trail trailhead near the parking area
Distance: 1.7-mile clockwise loop
Approximate hiking time: 1.5 hours
Difficulty: Easy due to flat surface
Trail surface: Dirt, grass
Best season: Year-round
Other trail users: Dog walkers, bird–watchers. Portions of the trail are wheelchair and stroller accessible.
Canine compatibility: Leashed dogs permitted
Fees and permits: None required
Schedule: Dawn to dusk
Maps: USGS: Antioch; trail maps available at office and online at www.tn.gov/agriculture
Trail contact: Manager, Ellington Agricultural Center, 440 Hogan Rd., Nashville, TN 37220; Phone: (615) 837-5103; www.tn.gov/agriculture
Other: There is no potable water or restrooms on the trail. Take adequate drinking water, and use sunscreen and insect repellant.

Finding the trailhead: From the south side of Nashville, take I-40 East/I-65 South via the ramp on the left toward Knoxville. Go 0.9 mile, then merge onto I-65 South via exit 210 toward Huntsville and proceed 4.3 miles. Take TN 255 at exit 78B and go 0.2 mile. After that, make a slight right onto Harding Place/TN 255, then turn left onto Franklin Road (US 31/TN 6). Turn left onto Hogan Road, and reach 440 Hogan Road. Proceed to the parking area. *Note:* Hogan Road ends at the Ellington Agricultural Center's front gate. *DeLorme Tennessee Atlas & Gazetteer:* Page 53, D5. GPS: N36 03.74' / W86 44.77'

This hike passes woodlands, meadows, and creeks throughout a 207-acre area that hosts 124 bird species. Start at the Eagle Trail trailhead adjoining the parking area and head west. The Eagle Trail leads through the Iris Garden and connects to Roberts Walk. The hike goes in a clockwise direction. Portions of the trail are wheelchair and stroller accessible, especially those through the campus.

Follow the 400-foot-long Eagle Trail as it heads downhill into the Bicentennial Iris Garden. These are formal gardens with benches and flowing water that create

The small bubbling rapids on Seven Mile Creek beckon the hiker for a short out and back on Roberts Trail.

a visual display not normally seen on a hike. Reach the Roberts Walk sign and follow the mulched path on the left side of the road. Pass a small hill on the right that slopes up about 25 feet. The Agricultural Center buildings are situated on the top of the hill. Bend right and cross over two sections of paved brick.

The trail widens and after bearing right leads into a large open meadow. The meadow is about 350 feet across and covers ten acres. Follow the trail along the park boundary, bordered on the left by Seven Mile Creek. Residences can be seen on the other side of the creek. Along the creek in the spring you'll find a profusion of yellow-blossomed forsythia bushes surrounded by yellow and white daffodils. These flowers and shrubs appear to be wild. Reach a path on the left that leads down to the creek. At the end of the path are small, gurgling rapids that create a great photo op. Watch for purple martins swooping low over the meadow on the right, scooping up insects, along with bluebirds and red-winged blackbirds flying around the trees that border the creek. Water bars have been placed at various points on the trail to help prevent erosion.

Several power transmission posts are at the north end of the meadow. Although the posts are not very attractive, they furnish platforms for red-tailed hawks to watch for unsuspecting prey, including birds, small mammals, and snakes. The trail surface is still dirt and flat. Bear right at the transmission posts, heading generally east. Head into the woods as the trail wanders to the right and left between the trees. Many birds can be heard and seen, including sparrows, yellowthroats, and the small, but beautiful, indigo bunting. Follow the trail, which may be muddy after a rain, as it heads slightly up. The Agricultural Center boundary fence is on the left, and the unseen campus on the right.

Green Tip:
Observe wildlife from a distance. Do not bend or break off tree branches to "get a better picture." This frightens wildlife and may destroy part of their camouflage.

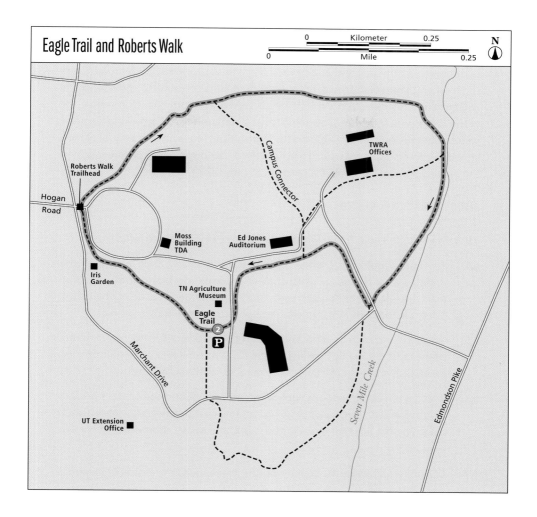

Eagle Trail and Roberts Walk

Continue following the trail through the woods as it slopes gradually up toward the hilltop. Small bushes edge both sides of the trail and furnish habitat for several species of birds and butterflies. Large mature trees, including sugar maple, black walnut, and hackberry, are favorites for migrating warblers, especially during the spring. In the fall look on the ground for walnuts that have dropped from the black walnut trees. Their shells will originally be green, turning to black as they ripen. They have a distinct smell, and the black shell can stain hands. The trail begins to flatten as it reaches the top of the hill. This portion of the hike is very relaxing and is a good spot to add an extra dimension to the hike by identifying birds or trees with the help of a guidebook.

Continue following the trail south and slightly up. An Agricultural Center boundary fence is on the left. Pass a path on the right that leads through some shrubs to the campus. This path may be taken to shorten the hike. Reach two posts in the center of the trail and just beyond them an Agricultural Center road. Cross the road and immediately turn right, onto the Campus Connector path, which is wheelchair and stroller accessible. It heads west and slightly up, along the edge of the campus on the left. Follow the path as it turns left across a parking area and various campus buildings, including the Agricultural Museum and several old log structures. This is a good spot for history buffs to spend some time before reaching the parking area for the Eagle Trail and ending the hike.

MILES AND DIRECTIONS

0.0 Start at the Eagle Trail trailhead near the parking area and head west.

0.1 Pass through the Iris Garden on the very short Eagle Trail, leading to the Roberts Walk trailhead, which has an information board and large trail map. Go left, heading northwest on the trail paralleling the asphalt road. Continue following the mulched trail slightly to the right.

0.3 Go down and then up a bricked area. The Agricultural Center buildings are to the right but nearly hidden by a hill. Continue following the trail, bearing northeast, and pass the Campus Connector path on the right.

0.5 Reach a ten-acre meadow, with Seven Mile Creek and the center's boundary on the left. Continue following the trail as it parallels the creek. Reach a path on the left that leads to the creek, and take a short out and back to explore the rapids.

0.7 Continue following the trail along the creek, heading east and toward a line of power transmission poles. The creek is on the left and the meadow is on the right.

0.9 Reach the transmission poles and make a hard right, heading south. Heavy woods are on the left and the meadow is on the right. Follow the trail for about 200 feet along the transmission poles and enter the woods.

1.2 Continuing following the trail south and slightly up. An Agricultural Center boundary fence is on the left. Pass a path on the right that leads to the campus and can be taken to shorten the hike.

1.3 Reach two posts in the center of the trail and then an Agricultural Center road. Cross the road and immediately turn right onto the Campus Connector path, which heads west and slightly up along the edge of the campus on the left. Follow the path as it turns left, passing various campus buildings.

1.7 Return to the trailhead and parking area.

Edwin Warner Park: Geology Trail

The Geology Trail combines portions of the Little Acorn, Nature Loop, and Harpeth Woods Trails so you can experience the best of Edwin Warner Park. A bridge behind the nature center leads to woods filled with a variety of hardwood trees, and another bridge over Vaughn's Creek offers good photo ops. Climb up the limestone outcrops to the high point of the hike, an abandoned quarry that is the turnaround point.

Start: Geology Trail trailhead, behind the nature center
Distance: 2.3 miles out and back
Approximate hiking time: 1.5 hours
Difficulty: Moderate due to some limestone outcrops
Trail surface: Dirt, rock
Best season: Year-round
Other trail users: Dog walkers
Canine compatibility: Leashed dogs permitted
Fees and permits: None required
Schedule: Dawn to dusk

Maps: USGS: Bellevue; trail maps and brochures available at nature center and trailhead
Trail contact: Warner Park Nature Center, 7311 TN 100, Nashville, TN 37221; (615) 352-6299; www.nashville.gov/parks/wpnc
Other: Restrooms and water are available at the nature center. There is no potable water or restrooms on the trail. Take adequate drinking water, and use sunscreen and insect repellant.

Finding the trailhead: From the south side of Nashville, take I-40 West toward Memphis for 9.2 miles to exit 99. Turn left onto Old Hickory Boulevard/TN 251 and follow Old Hickory for 3.8 miles. Turn left onto TN 100, follow it 0.6 mile to Edwin Warner Park, and proceed to the nature center. *DeLorme Tennessee Atlas & Gazetteer:* Page 53, C5. GPS: N36 03.58' / W86 54.74'

3

THE HIKE

This hike is an out and back, heading west and south to an abandoned quarry and then returning. Much of the hike parallels Vaughn's Creek and passes woodlands, meadows, and limestone outcrops as it leads to the quarry.

Before your hike, stop at the nature center and pick up a trail map and interpretive brochure for the Geology Trail. Start at the kiosk near the rear of the nature center. Notice the pond, plantings, and buildings used by the center's personnel for teaching and demonstrations. Immediately cross a bridge over Vaughn's Creek and

Limestone "steps" help in going up slopes on the Geology Trail in Edwin Warner Park.

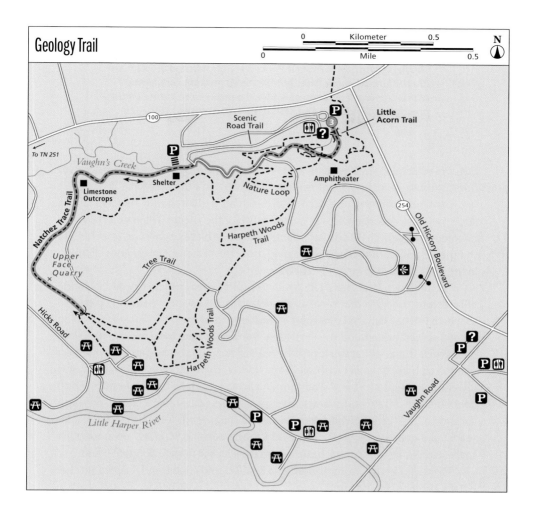

turn right onto the Little Acorn Trail; the creek is on the right. Watch for the green blazes on the trees identifying the Little Acorn Trail. This section is only 75 yards long and leads to a bridge that connects to the Nature Loop Trail, which is identified by yellow blazes on the trees. The creek now is on the left, with dense woods and undergrowth reaching to the trail's edge.

Pass a path on the right leading to a children's play area and the nature center, then cross a bridge and make a hard right at the end of it. Continue following the trail in a westerly direction while trying to identify some of the large hardwood trees in the woods, including oaks, hickories and maples. Go down a few steps to reach the park road and follow the road as it branches to the right. Portions of the road are part of the Tree Trail and have signs identifying various tree species. The low rock wall you see was built by the Civilian Conservation Corps (CCC) in the 1930s. The

> *The Percy and Edwin Warner Parks were established in 1927 and are the largest municipally administered parks in Tennessee, with a combined acreage of 2,684. The parks were placed on the prestigious Tennessee Register of Natural Areas in 1980.*

CCC was established by President Franklin Roosevelt during the Great Depression to furnish employment for young men aged late teens to early twenties.

Continue following the road until reaching a shelter with benches and a large trail map. A parking area is located north of the shelter. The trail, which now becomes the Harpeth Woods Trail, identified by blue blazes, continues from behind the shelter and leads to a bridge crossing the creek. Watch for large vines climbing in the trees while following the trail west.

The trail then bears hard left, heading south toward the quarry and a hillside of limestone outcrops that serve as nature's steps. This section heading up the hill to where the trail flattens is the most strenuous part of the hike. Zig and zag, going up and sometimes around the limestone. The woods here have more cedars than hardwoods. Turn right at the top of the hill, still heading south. Watch for numbers painted on rocks that refer to the Geology Trail interpretive guide. Follow the trail as it weaves through rocks and woods until reaching a Y. Take the left branch, which continues straight ahead, leading to the upper edges of the quarry. Listen and watch for birds, as the height of the ridge and surrounding woods furnish ideal habitat for scarlet tanagers and cardinals. These ridges, approaching 800 feet, are among the highest in Tennessee's central basin, where the average ridge is about 550 feet.

The trail veers left, right, and left as it heads slightly down and reaches another Y. Take the right branch and head down, passing a park bench. Six steps aid in reducing the grade down to the quarry floor, which may be swampy after a rain. Inspect the various rock layers in the walls of the quarry, and use the interpretive guide to find explanations of the geological features. Spend some time investigating the quarry and its geological history before backtracking to the trailhead.

MILES AND DIRECTIONS

0.0   Start at the Geology Trail trailhead, at the kiosk at the rear of the nature center. Within 200 feet cross a bridge over Vaughn's Creek and turn right onto the Little Acorn Trail (marked with green blazes on trees), which borders the creek and ends at a bridge.

0.1   Cross the bridge and connect with the Nature Loop Trail (marked with yellow blazes), heading south and immediately west, with the creek on the left.

0.2 Pass a trail marker post and reach a T; take the left branch, continuing on the Nature Loop Trail. Cross a bridge and take a hard right. The trail veers right, left, and right and within 200 feet crosses another bridge. (**Note:** The trail zigs, zags, and even doubles back on itself, but the path is clear and it continues to head generally west and south.)

0.4 Continue following the trail in a generally west direction to five log steps that lead up to a park road. Follow along the walking space at the edge of the road until it branches. Take the right branch, still heading west.

0.6 Reach a gate across the road and bear left to reach a small shelter that has a large park trail map. Turn left at the rear of the shelter and head toward the creek. Bear slightly left and cross a bridge to reach the Harpeth Woods Trail (marked with blue blazes). This is part of the Geology Trail.

0.8 Reach a marker post and large stones across the trail. Turn right, continuing on the Harpeth Woods Trail south toward the quarry.

0.9 Follow the trail as it makes a hard left, heading south over some limestone outcrops that serve as steps. This is the most strenuous section of the hike. The trail doubles back for a short section.

1.15 Reach a Y and take the left branch, heading south. Continue straight for about 400 feet and reach another Y; take the right branch going down six steps to the quarry. The trail weaves right, left, and back right, still heading generally south by southeast. Proceed a few hundred feet to reach the quarry. Turn around and backtrack to the trailhead.

2.3 End the hike at the trailhead.

More Precious than Gold

The hilly area around Dickson, in Dickson County, about 40 miles east of Nashville, once contained a treasure more precious than gold. It was iron ore, and around 1800 it lured workers to middle Tennessee by the hundreds, attracted by the high pay offered for the back-breaking job of mining it. The man responsible for building the iron industry in middle Tennessee was Montgomery Bell, whose foundry furnished cannonballs used in the War of 1812.

The iron ore was dug from the ground, creating pits that are still visible today, and trees in the surrounding hardwood forest were cut to furnish the charcoal necessary for the smelting process. The remains of the old Laurel Furnace can be seen in Montgomery Bell State Park.

Bell searched for a place to build a water-powered mill and discovered a spot on the nearby Harpeth River that formed a steep bend, almost doubling back on itself. The two sections of the river flowed around a narrow but steep hill, with one section being several feet lower than the other. Those river sections covered 5 miles, but a person could walk over the hill in half an hour. Bell used some engineering creativity and determined that if a tunnel could be dug through the dirt and limestone, the river could be diverted to furnish the power the mill needed.

Slaves started boring the hole in 1819. When completed, the hole was 8 feet deep, 16 feet wide, and 290 feet long. It was a monumental work, requiring a great deal of slave labor, and it was, incidentally, very picturesque. The ironworks are long gone, but the pool created by outflow from the tunnel still exists. Hikers use it to wade in the river and cool off.

It has taken the better part of a century for the forests to fully recover. The federal government, under the direction of President Franklin D. Roosevelt, created demonstration projects during the 1930s and 1940s to help restore the land. These wounds are now healed, allowing foxes, deer, raccoons, squirrels, and many species of birds to call the area home. It is also great hiking country. The Bowie Woods: Bowie Lakes Loop (hike 31) is the closest hike in this guidebook to the area; but many hikers like to take this hike, then go east to the ironworks site.

4

Edwin Warner Park: Scenic Road Trail

The Scenic Road Trail takes you back to the days when Edwin Warner Park opened in 1927, when touring cars and bus trips were popular ways to see the park. Wind up and down through wooded areas and valleys, and to the park's boundary at Old Hickory Boulevard. A portion of the trail overlaps the Tree Trail, which has informational signs describing various trees. The low stone wall that borders part of the trail was built by the Civilian Conservation Corps (CCC) in the 1930s.

Start: Scenic Road Trail trailhead by the nature center
Distance: 3.3-mile lollipop
Approximate hiking time: 2 hours
Difficulty: Moderate due to the narrow trail and some steep inclines
Trail surface: Dirt, asphalt road
Best season: Year-round
Other trail users: Joggers, dog walkers
Canine compatibility: Leashed dogs permitted
Fees and permits: None required

Schedule: 8:00 a.m. to 5:00 p.m.
Maps: USGS: Bellevue; trail maps and brochures available at nature center
Trail contact: Warner Park Nature Center, 7311 TN 100, Nashville, TN 37221; (615) 352-6299; www .nashville.gov/parks/wpnc
Other: Restrooms and water are available at the nature center. There is no potable water or restrooms on the trail. Take adequate drinking water, and use sunscreen and insect repellant.

Finding the trailhead: From the south side of Nashville, take I-40 West toward Memphis for 9.2 miles to exit 99. Turn left onto Old Hickory Boulevard/TN 251 and follow Old Hickory for 3.8 miles. Turn left onto TN 100, follow it 0.6 mile to Edwin Warner Park, and proceed to the nature center. *DeLorme Tennessee Atlas & Gazetteer:* Page 53, C5. GPS: N36 03.59' / W86 54.74'

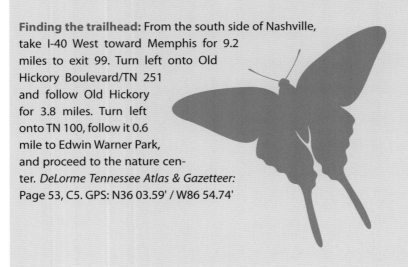

Sections of several trails, including the Old Roadway Scenic Tree Trail, have been combined to cover much of Edwin Warner Park in this hike. The hike is a lollipop, starting west and then heading east and south until reaching the beginning of the clockwise loop. Benches are conveniently placed along the trail.

Before your hike, stop at the nature center and pick up a trail map and interpretive brochure. From the nature center, follow the road (which is closed to vehicular traffic) west to a shelter containing benches and a large map; this is the trailhead

The Scenic Trail in Edwin Warner Park features a number of interesting trees, many of which are identified by labels.

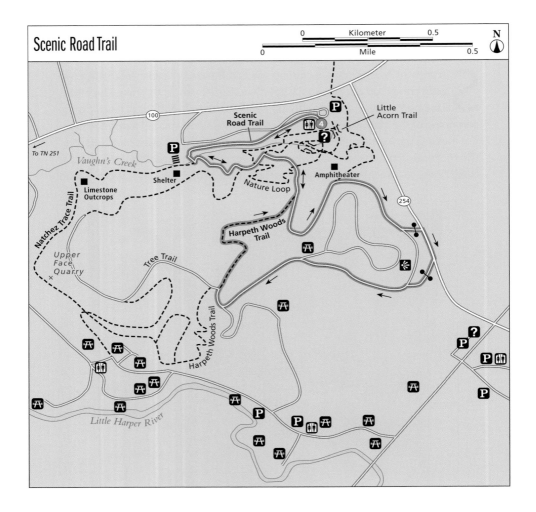

for the Natchez Trace Trail, which leads to the quarry. Follow the road behind the shelter, heading generally west, and notice the low stone wall bordering the road. It was constructed in the 1930s by the Civilian Conservation Corps (CCC), which was established by President Franklin D. Roosevelt during the Great Depression to furnish jobs to young men. Much of their work was done in state parks.

Numerous gray smooth-barked beech trees are sprinkled throughout the woods. The beech is one of the few trees that holds its leaves through the winter. The beeches prefer the drier hillsides, away from the creek, which is on the left. In the spring notice wildflowers such as noncultivated yellow and white jonquils and daffodils. Pass a path on the right that leads to the Nature Loop Trail, which is identified with yellow blazes. Follow the road as it bears right and heads south. The woods are filled with a variety of trees, including hickory, bur oak, sycamore,

. blah

elm, and tulip poplar. Add an extra dimension to your hike by using the Tree Trail pamphlet for this portion of the route.

At the Y in the road take the left branch, heading east. Follow the road as it forms a semicircle, passing a rustic park bench and then paralleling the previous section of the trail. An interesting gully lies between the two sections of road, and in the spring it is filled with wildflowers. Follow the road, now generally south, to a large observation platform. The platform offers some panoramic views and is a good spot to rest. Leave the observation deck and follow the road to the right, heading toward Old Hickory Boulevard.

Soon you reach a gate across the road, with a dirt path on the right labeled the Paved Road Connector Trail. Take this narrow path, which weaves up a fairly steep hill, through the trees, and along some limestone outcrops. Follow the trail down to where it reconnects to the Scenic Road Trail. Take a right on the road as it heads south and continue going west, following the terrain up and down. Notice the mixture of woods and grassy areas on the right and left. The road leads generally west to a three-way intersection, with a path leading to a shelter across the road.

At the intersection follow the center road, which slopes up and down, then flattens and continues west. Try to identify the various tree species, including flowering dogwood, with its showy white petals in the spring and red berries, and red leaves in the fall. In a short distance reach a Y; take the right branch as it heads toward the blue-blazed Harpeth Woods Trail and the yellow-blazed Nature Loop Trail. Notice the black walnut trees with their deeply grooved bark and narrow leaves. In the fall look for the ball-shaped, green-husked nuts.

Pass a path on the left that leads to a shelter. Continue following the Harpeth Woods Trail up and down through the woods until reaching a T. Take the right branch and bear right, then double back, bear left, and double back again. This is an interesting section of the hike. The left branch leads to a bridge and a large limestone outcrop. Follow the trail as it crosses the road by the shelter and Natchez Trace trailhead, then backtrack to the nature center to end the hike.

MILES AND DIRECTIONS

0.0 Start at the nature center and head west to the Scenic Road Trail.

0.1 Follow the park road west. The road was once the old touring road, but vehicular traffic is no longer allowed.

0.2 Reach a T in the road and take the left branch, heading generally southeast. Pass a path on the right that leads to the Nature Loop Trail. Continue following the road, heading east. **(Note:** The hike is a lollipop, but the trail zigs, zags, and even doubles back on itself, so that at any time the hike description, miles and directions, or map could go in an opposite direction for a short distance.) After the road section, the trail continually weaves, often in very short stretches, among the trees.

0.3 Follow the road to a T and take the right branch. Cross a section of the Nature Loop Trail. Continue following the road to the right, heading east.

0.5 Reach a Y in the road and take the left branch, which loops around to parallel the trail you came from. There is a gully between the two segments of the road. Continue north and pass the amphitheater and a large hardwood on the left, with a 5- to 6-foot-diameter trunk.

0.9 Reach a large wood observation deck. A narrow path ends at the edge of the deck; this is the terminus of the short Hungry Hawk Trail. Return to the road and continue following it west, then north.

1.0 Reach a gate blocking the Scenic Road from entering Old Hickory Boulevard. Follow just past the gate to reach a dirt connector path on the right, marked by two large stones. Follow this path, which heads up into the woods.

1.3 The trail flattens and then heads down to the Scenic Road. Turn right onto the road, heading south, and follow it slightly to the right and up.

1.8 Continue following the Scenic Road until reaching a three-way intersection. Take the left branch, heading west. A picnic shelter is located just beyond the T.

1.9 Follow the road until reaching a Y. Take the right branch, which also heads toward the Nature Loop and Harpeth Woods Trail.

2.2 Continue following the road; this portion is also part of the Tree Trail and has small signs identifying the various species. Reach a dirt trail on the right. Leave the road and take the trail, following to the right. This is the Harpeth Woods Trail, marked with blue blazes.

2.3 Follow the trail in a generally north direction as it weaves through the woods and doubles back on itself two times.

2.6 Pass a bench on the left and bear right, continuing downhill and heading northeast.

2.9 Reach a T and take the left branch. Bear right and then hard left, as the trail doubles back on itself. This section of the trail serves as both the Nature Loop and Harpeth Woods Trail. Continue following the trail as it weaves back and forth through the woods.

3.1 Reach an intersection with a marker post with a green blaze pointing left. Take the left branch onto the Little Acorn Trail. Bear right in a tight semi-circle until reaching a creek. Follow the creek a short distance and turn hard left to reach a bridge. Cross the bridge, taking a hard right at the end, and cross a mowed area to reach the nature center.

3.3 End the hike at the trailhead.

Spiders Are Not Scary

While visiting my daughter and her family one day, I went out on the porch with my seven-year-old granddaughter Samantha Jo (who everybody calls Sammy) and noticed a large spider web hanging from the corner of the porch ceiling. "Sammy," I said, "why don't you have your dad brush that spider web away? Spiders are scary."

I've had an arm's-length attitude toward spiders since I was a young boy and read that naturalist John Muir died from the bite of a brown recluse spider. Also, walking into their webs across a trail has never engendered any kind feelings.

Sammy quickly answered. "Spiders are not scary! Well, when my mommy and I first saw the spider, I was a little afraid. But now, Briana is my friend!" Taken aback, I said, "You've named the spider? How do you know it's a she?" She replied, "Because my daddy saw it was having a baby and told me." I asked her what she did then. She told me that every day she and her dad or mom watched the spider. "Daddy told me a lot of things about spiders." I asked if she knew what kind of spider it was. I was informed that the spider was an orb weaver. I suggested that maybe we should go back to the porch and investigate Briana.

The web was flat, ornate, and circular, the common type normally associated with spiders. "Look, Grandpa," Sammy said. "She has really long legs." I looked more closely and noticed that her body was about an inch long, but her legs were much longer. The spider was brightly colored, marked with yellow, black, and orange. The spider—that is, Briana—did not move much while we were observing her. I moved to place my finger on the web to see what it felt like. Sammy's response to my action was quick, "Don't touch her web, Grandpa, because she gets very upset." She asked me to move away from the web so she could show me how Briana was not afraid of her.

I watched as I moved back on the porch. Sammy moved slowly toward the web and then just stood there, motionless. In about a minute, though it seemed much longer, Briana slowly came down the web toward Sammy. I had to control myself to keep from yelling, "Sammy, that's amazing!" I never thought I would be watching a spider coming down a web toward my granddaughter without dispatching the spider. I asked Sammy if she had time to help me do a little Internet searching to get more information about spiders.

Our first search was to find a little more about orb weavers. We found out that orb weavers are also known as the black and yellow garden spider. The thick interwoven section in the web's center has also led to them being called the writing spider. We continued on the website and learned that the male is often less than one-quarter the size of the female and is normally not in the same web as the female. Orb weavers are harmless but can be a nuisance when they build their large webs across trails and other places inconvenient to humans.

The website reminded us that most spiders are small, inconspicuous arthropods and are harmless to humans. This caused Sammy to ask, "What's an arthropod?" I told her it means insects and spiders with jointed legs. We found out there are over one hundred species of spiders in Tennessee and that only the brown recluse and black widow are considered venomous to humans. We skipped down to black widows and were surprised to learn that contrary to popular belief, southern black widow female spiders do not eat their mates after mating. This is not true of their relatives to the north, where the clan got its name.

Thanks to Sammy, my concern over spiders was a thing of the past.

Don't look for a springhouse on this trail—it is a lost piece of history. The narrow dirt trail follows up and down through heavy woods until reaching Two Rivers Lake. Fishermen may be seen testing their skills, while turtles sun themselves on logs. Wildflowers are abundant in spring.

Start: McGavock Springhouse Trail trailhead adjacent to kiosk in parking area

Distance: 1.3 miles out and back

Approximate hiking time: 1.5 hours

Difficulty: Moderate due to narrow dirt trail and up-and-down slopes

Trail surface: Dirt

Best season: September to June

Other trail users: Dog walkers

Canine compatibility: Leashed dogs permitted

Fees and permits: None required

Schedule: Dawn to dusk

Maps: USGS: Nashville East; map board at trailhead kiosk

Trail contact: Nashville Metropolitan Board of Parks and Recreation, P.O. Box 196340, Nashville, TN 37219; (615) 862-8400; www .greenwaysfornashville.org

Other: Water and restrooms are available near the parking area. There is no potable water or restrooms on the trail. Take adequate drinking water, and use sunscreen and insect repellant.

Finding the trailhead: From the southwest side of Nashville, take I-40 East via the ramp on the left toward Knoxville. Go 6 miles, then merge onto Briley Parkway via exit 215B and proceed 1.9 miles. Take the Lebanon Pike/US 70 exit (exit 8) toward Donelson and go 0.3 mile. Turn right on Lebanon Pike/US 70 and proceed 0.3 mile. Turn left onto McGavock Pike and go 2 miles to the second 2 Rivers Parkway on the left. Turn into Two Rivers Park and proceed to the parking area and kiosk for the trail. *DeLorme Tennessee Atlas & Gazetteer:* Page 53, C5. GPS: N36 11.52' / W86 40.67'

This trail is in Two Rivers Park, with the Cumberland River circling the north end, and is a section of the Stones River Greenway. (The Stones River joins the Cumberland east of the park.) The out-and-back hike heads steeply down through heavy woods until reaching the lake, where the trail flattens. The trail is dirt and can be muddy and slippery after a rain.

Begin at the McGavock Spring House Trail trailhead adjacent to the kiosk and map in the parking area. Cross the road, using caution, and head into the woods, going north and following the 2-foot-wide dirt trail. The trees are hardwood and include oak, maple, and willow. There are many vines along both sides of the trail, some of them crossing it. A few of the vines have long, sharp, and potentially dangerous thorns—use caution to avoid them. Bushes also border the trail, furnishing habitat for small birds and butterflies. The birds can be heard, but are rarely seen. Continue heading sharply down, as the trail zigzags right, left, and then right again. Even with all this meandering, the trail is heading north.

Continue heading down, using a few limestone "steps" to help in the descent. Bear hard right, then left, and cross a rickety bridge over a seasonal creek. The large

The McGavock Spring House Trail leads by a meandering unnamed creek. This trail is a part of the Stones River Greenway.

(approximately 8 by 10 feet and 2 feet high) flat-surfaced limestone rock you pass is a great spot to rest and enjoy the woods. Bear left after the bridge and then hard right, still heading north. At the bottom of the hill you arrive at a small clearing. This part of the trail has good canopy cover. An unnamed body of water is to the left, probably a meander of the Cumberland River. Willow trees grow at its edge, and several trees have toppled into the water. This section of the hike has covered less than 1,200 feet—simply amazing!

The entire character of the hike changes at this point. The woods are replaced by a few trees, with the lake on the left and mowed grass and low hills on the right. The trail nearly disappears into the grass as it heads northwest, bordering the lakeshore. A few anglers can usually be seen trying their luck. There are many clearings down to the lake, affording the opportunity to investigate its edge. This area is turtle paradise, with the calm water and half-sunken logs reaching back to the shore. Most of the turtles are red-eared sliders, and they are present in all seasons except winter—it's not unusual to see eight to ten of them on one log. They slide into the water when they feel vibrations from footsteps.

The water's edge is a great place to look for animal tracks, bird tracks, and aquatic creatures. Common visitors to the lake's edge are raccoons, white-tailed deer, coyotes, and an occasional great blue heron. Look carefully at water plants for frogs resting and looking for a meal. Often just a splash is seen, as the frog dives into the water. Water striders and mayflies are also present. Water snakes call this area home, but are seldom seen. After investigating the riparian habitat, turn right and head up the hill.

It may be necessary to chart your own trail up the hill to the park road, heading north. The top of the hill affords a sweeping view of the area, including the river, a small impoundment, and a golf course. Walk a short distance along the road, then return down the hill and bear right, heading nearly west. Bear right a short distance toward a picnic table and a small bluff containing some limestone outcrops. This is a good spot to rest and enjoy the solitude before backtracking to the trailhead.

MILES AND DIRECTIONS

0.0 Start at the kiosk adjoining the Two Rivers Park parking area. Cross the road and head north.

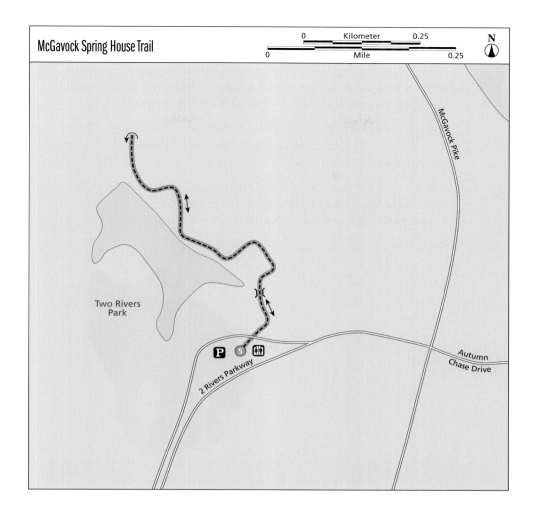

0.1 Follow the narrow trail into the woods as it zigzags and slopes down toward a meander of the Cumberland River. Some sections are quite steep and can be muddy after a rain. Cross a bridge over a seasonal creek. Bear left at the end of the bridge, heading slightly west for a very short distance, and then take a hard right. A portion of the Cumberland meander can be seen on the left as the trail flattens.

0.2 Reach the edge of the lake and take a hard right, following along the water and heading northwest.

0.3 Bear left and then right as the trail parallels the lake on the left and dense woods on the right, still heading generally northwest. Reach an opening, with the lake still on the left and a small hill on the right. Follow along the lakeshore, heading northwest, and then bear right to head up the hill.

0.4 Reach the top of the hill and a park road. Follow along the park road, heading mostly northwest. Turn left coming down the hill, heading southwest, down to the lake.

0.65 Follow along the shoreline and then bear right, heading northeast for a short distance, and reach a picnic table, facing a bluff. Go diagonally, heading southeast back to the lake, and backtrack to the trailhead.

1.3 End the hike at the trailhead.

Nashville's Greenways

With 36.5 miles of trail, Nashville's greenways run primarily along major rivers and creeks. They feature several large nature parks and passive recreation areas, including the Stones River Greenway, a 65-acre parcel through which the McGavock Spring House Trail (hike 5) runs, the 810-acre Shelby Bottoms Greenway, 1,500-acre Beaman Park (hike 7), and 800-acre Bells Bend Park (hike 8). A new bridge over the Cumberland River links the Stones River Greenway to Shelby Bottoms at Two Rivers Parkway. In time, the goal is to connect the Stones River Greenway in Nashville to the Murfreesboro Greenway, creating an uninterrupted trail between the two cities, a distance of some 30 miles.

Mill Creek Greenway Trail

This in-city hike is especially convenient for the folks in Antioch. It takes you around Antioch Middle School, the community center, and then along Mill Creek. Watch for birds and other wildlife near the creek's edge. The shallow, nearly pristine creek and woods bordering it provide good habitat for wildlife in this residential area.

Start: Mill Creek Greenway Trail trailhead adjacent to the Antioch Community Center parking area

Distance: 3 miles out and back

Approximate hiking time: 1.5 hours

Difficulty: Easy due to paved surface and shade

Trail surface: Asphalt

Best season: Year-round

Other trail users: Bicyclists, strollers, wheelchairs, joggers, dog walkers

Canine compatibility: Leashed dogs permitted

Fees and permits: None required

Schedule: Dawn to dusk

Maps: USGS: Antioch; large map board at trailhead

Trail contact: Antioch Parks and Recreation, 1523 New Hall Rd., Antioch, TN 37013; (615) 315-9363; www.greenwaysfornashville.org

Other: Water and restrooms are available in the Antioch Community Center, and the parking area has a porta-potty. There is no potable water or restrooms on the trail. Take adequate water and use insect repellant and sunscreen, as much of the trail lacks any tree cover.

Finding the trailhead: From the west side of Nashville, take I-40 East via the ramp on the left and go 4 miles toward Knoxville. Keep right to take I-24 East via exit 213A toward Chattanooga and go 5.7 miles. Take the East Haywood Lane exit (exit 57B) toward Antioch and go 0.2 mile. Merge onto Haywood Lane and go 0.3 mile, then turn right onto Antioch Pike and go 1 mile. Turn right onto Blue Hole Road and go 0.2 mile to 5023 Blue Hole Rd., Antioch, on the right. *DeLorme Tennessee Atlas & Gazetteer:* Page 53, D4. N36 03.26' W86 40.24'

The Mill Creek Greenway is one of many greenways in the Nashville area. The ultimate plan is to connect as many as possible in order to furnish recreational opportunities for a large part of the population. Much of the land used for many of the greenways provide local flood control and are considered inappropriate for any other use. There are plans afoot to lengthen the Mill Creek Greenway Trail by continuing it to Ezell Park and adding a loop to it. Contact the Antioch Parks and Recreation Department for more information.

The hike starts at the trailhead adjacent to the parking area at the Antioch Community Center. This is a wide, paved, multiuse trail, accessible to wheelchairs

The clear, shallow, nearly pristine Mill Creek borders the Mill Creek Trail. Rapids and limestone outcrops add to the visual display.

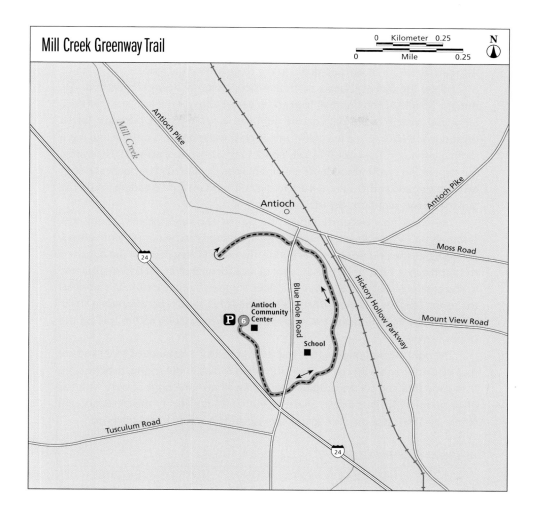

and strollers, so keep to the right and be aware of joggers, bicyclists (who sometimes approach like stealth aircraft), and dog walkers. A large map board at the trailhead lists various checkpoints along the trail. This is an out-and-back hike that follows south, then northeast, then north, then west, and backtracks to the trailhead. Several long benches are built into a fence on the outgoing right side of the trail, providing opportunities to kick back. I-24 is to the left and can be noisy.

Head south from the trailhead, away from the community center and toward Antioch Middle School. Pass around the south end of the school, with the buildings on the left, separated from the trail by a chain-link fence. The trail slopes slightly down toward Mill Creek, heading northeast. Notice the trees and small shrubs bordering the creek, which is on the right. A sitting area built in as part of a fence will be on the right. The fence, which is about 40 feet long, discourages folks from going down to the creek. Almost immediately, you'll pass another sitting area on the right. There is a sharp drop down to the creek behind the fence.

Follow the trail as it bears north and slopes slightly down and flattens. The Antioch Middle School football field and bleachers are on the left. In a short distance you come to a dirt path on the right that leads to a creek overlook. Take a short out and back to see the creek, whose clear water appears pristine and has a slight bluish tinge. The creek is usually about 12 to 20 inches deep and 50 feet wide, but depending on the amount of rainfall, it may be dry. Railroad tracks can be seen on the other side of the creek. Return to the trail and turn right, heading north. The trail then bears slightly to the left.

The creek now becomes hidden by shrubs and undergrowth as the trail slopes slightly down. Bear left, heading west; a bridge can be seen straight ahead. As you reach the underpass for the bridge, the creek is very close on the right and the approach is flat. This is the best spot to look for animal tracks and small creek-loving creatures. Raccoons, opossums, deer, squirrels, and other animals come to the water. Frogs and water striders call the creek home, and occasionally a snake may be seen. Return to the trail and cross under the bridge to the trail on the opposite side.

The right and left edges of the trail are mowed for a distance of 4 feet and are met by shrubs and a few trees. Birds, including robins in the spring, may be seen flying and foraging on the ground. Reach a T and take the right branch, with the creek on the right. Pass a path on the right that leads down to the creek, about 8 feet away. This is a good place to turn around and backtrack to the trailhead.

MILES AND DIRECTIONS

0.0 Start at the trailhead adjacent to the Antioch Community Center parking area. Head south toward Antioch Middle School and turn left (northeast).

Local lore has it that Mill Creek was named for the gristmills that residents established along the creek to grind grain into flour.

0.1 Follow the paved trail between the middle school on the left and residences on the right, then bear hard left around the school. Continue following the paved trail north, with the school campus on the left, bordered on the right by a chain-link fence and Mill Creek (not visible).

0.4. Pass a rail fence on the right that has a sitting area built onto it. Continue following the asphalt trail north and pass another sitting area on the right.

0.5 Pass a sitting area that creates a fence on the right. The middle school football field is behind the fence on the left. Continue following the asphalt trail north.

0.7 Take a short dirt path on the right that leads to a Mill Creek overlook. Return to the main trail and bear slightly right, still heading north.

0.9 Follow the trail as it slopes down and goes under a bridge. Bear left at the end of the bridge, heading west. The creek is on the right. The trail weaves a bit but still goes west.

1.1 Reach a T and take the right branch, heading northwest and following along the creek.

1.5 Continue following the trail in a northwesterly direction along the creek. A path on the right leads down to the creek. This is a good spot to stop and backtrack to the trailhead.

3.0 End the hike at the trailhead.

> **🍃 Green Tip:**
> *When hiking with your dog, stay in the center of the path and keep Fido close by. Dogs that run loose can harm fragile soils and spread pesky plants by carrying their seeds.*

Beaman Park: Creekside Trail and Henry Hollow Loop

This is a great hike for bird-watchers and those who enjoy the sight of woods and limestone walls bordering creeks. The trail goes through rugged landscapes, including ridgetops nearly 1,000 feet high. Follow an edge of the western Highland Rim and watch for mountain laurel, wild azalea, and blueberries. Steep slopes, narrow hollows, woods, and streams create a constantly changing view.

Start: Creekside Trail trailhead next to the parking area
Distance: 3-mile clockwise loop
Approximate hiking time: 2.5 hours
Difficulty: Moderate due to some steep slopes
Trail surface: Dirt, rock
Best season: Year-round
Other trail users: Dog walkers, bird-watchers
Canine compatibility: Leashed dogs permitted
Fees and permits: None required
Schedule: Dawn to dusk

Maps: USGS: Forest Grove; trail maps available at nature center
Trail contact: Beaman Park Nature Center, 5911 Old Hickory Blvd., Ashland City, TN 37015; (615) 862-8580; www.nashville .gov/parks/nature
Other: A porta-potty is located by the parking area. There is no potable water or restrooms on the trail. Use insect repellant and take adequate water. The nature center is not open every day; call ahead for hours.

Finding the trailhead: From the southwest side of Nashville, take I-40 West toward Memphis and go 3.7 miles. Merge onto Briley Parkway via exit 204A and go 5.1 miles. Take TN 12 East via exit 24 and go 0.7 mile, then turn left onto Eatons Creek Road and go 4.2 miles. Cross Old Hickory Boulevard (turn left here for the nature center). In about 1 mile turn left onto Little Marrowbone Road. The Creekside Trail parking area and trailhead are on the left. *DeLorme Tennessee Atlas & Gazetteer:* Page 53, B5. GPS: N36 16.40' W86 54.29'

THE HIKE

This hike is a favorite of bird-watchers, wildflower seekers, creek lovers, dog walkers, and those just looking for a great hike. It forms a clockwise loop as it combines the Creekside Trail and Henry Hollow Loop to take in the best of 1,688-acre Beaman Park. The trail follows creeks and climbs up ridges, reaching a height of nearly 1,000 feet. It is situated on the Highland Rim, just outside the Nashville Basin, giving it a unique combination of flora and fauna.

The hike begins at the Creekside Trail trailhead, adjoining the kiosk and shelter next to the parking area. There is a large trail map and benches at the kiosk. Head east on the gravel path to a semicircular stone-floored overlook facing Henry Creek, and take a moment to enjoy the view. The creek is about 30 feet below. Head south from the overlook and immediately reach a Y. Take the left branch, which follows the Creekside Trail and joins the Henry Hollow Loop. At times the trails overlap, but watch for the white blazes.

The trail slopes down to the creek, which is on the left. It is about 15 feet wide, 6 to 10 inches deep, and crystal clear. Limestone walls are on the other side of the creek and "weep" after a rain. Look for gray smooth-barked beech trees in the woods, which hold their leaves through the winter. In the spring wildflowers,

There are several opportunities to ford the shallow Little Marrowbone Creek, on Creekside Trail in Beaman Park.

It may be difficult to imagine, but this land's early use included homesteads, farming, orchards, logging, and even moonshining. The purchase of the land for a park was made possible by a generous gift from Mrs. Sally Beaman in honor of her husband.

including wild geranium and dwarf larkspur, abound along the creek's banks. Summer features coreopsis, and fall brings forth blue lobelia and joe-pye weed. Several species of ferns also flourish along the creek.

The area's creeks, with their gurgling rapids and wildflower displays, are a high point of the hike. Look for yellow and rust-colored mudstone and for animal tracks, including deer, bobcat, coyote, and raccoon. Frogs, turtles, salamanders, and a few snakes also enjoy the riparian landscape. Young folks may enjoy looking for minnows and crayfish. This is ideal habitat for summer and scarlet tanagers during their breeding season, from April to late June.

Cross a bridge over a creek that joins Henry Creek at right angles. At the end of the bridge, head slightly up and step over some water bars across the trail, placed here to reduce erosion. The trail now leaves the creeks and heads into the ridges. Continue following the white blazes, heading up. The creek and bridge can be seen below. The woods contain mainly oak, but tulip poplars, a few cedars, and other species are interspersed. In the spring look for wild azaleas and mountain laurel, which are not common around Nashville, and in the summer look for blueberries.

Continue the climb to the top of the ridge as the trail veers right, left, and right again. Use caution, as there are steep slopes at the edge of the trail. The hike up is not difficult, but it is steady and long. Reach the crossover where the Henry Hollow Loop and Ridgetop Trail join. The junction is well marked. At this point the hike may be extended by taking the out-and-back Ridgetop Trail, adding 3.4 miles. Take the right branch to continue on the Henry Hollow Loop. The trails overlap for a short distance and are marked with both white and red blazes. Continue following the trail as it weaves through the trees, heading down.

Pass an unmarked trail on the right that leads to the Highland Trail trailhead and parking area. Continue following the trail as it weaves through the woods, generally heading north, for about 1 mile, with no landmarks, junctions, or paths intersecting it. Follow the trail, marked with white blazes, as it heads down, completing the loop. When you reach the Y (the Y you encountered at the beginning of the hike), take the left branch, backtracking the short distance to the trailhead.

Creekside Trail and Henry Hollow Loop

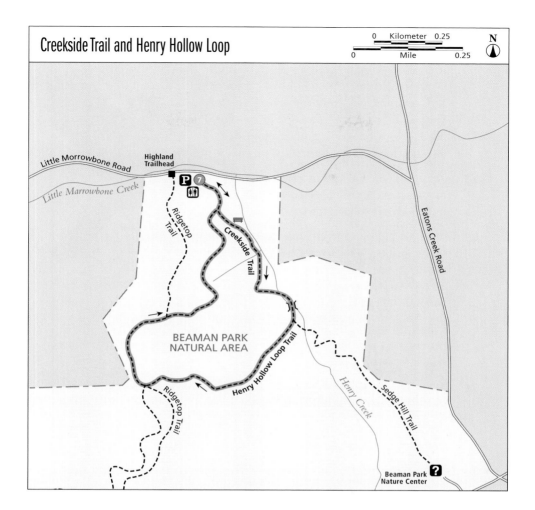

MILES AND DIRECTIONS

0.0   Start at the Creekside Trail trailhead and take the left branch, heading southeast.

0.1   Follow the trail down a slope to an observation overlook, with Little Marrowbone Creek about 30 feet below. Leave the overlook and immediately reach a Y (the distance from the trailhead to the Y is about 400 feet). Take the left branch, heading south. The Creekside Trail and Henry Hollow Loop, identified with white blazes on trees, share the same trail. Take an out and back on the path on the left that leads to the creek. Return to the trail, heading south.

0.2 Continue following the trail south as it borders Henry Creek, which is on the left side. Watch for white blazes on trees. **(Note:** Even though the trail is a clockwise loop, it zigs, zags, and may even double back on itself, so that any time the hike description, miles and directions, or map could go in an opposite direction for a short distance.)

0.4 Pass a path on the left that leads down to the creek. Continue following the trail south as it follows the creek.

0.5 Cross a bridge over an unnamed seasonal creek that intersects with Henry Creek. Head slightly uphill at the end of the bridge, temporarily going east. The creek is on the left. Bear right, heading south, and continue following the trail. Pass a path to the creek on the left.

0.7 Follow the trail south and slightly up to a T. Take the left branch and immediately cross a bridge. Make a hard right, then left as the trail flattens, now heading generally west. Continue following the trail as it zigs and zags.

1.0 As the trail heads up, notice a white blaze on the right. Bear right at the blaze, continuing up the slope.

1.4 Reach the top of the ridge and follow the trail as it heads down, bearing slightly left. Veer left as the trail flattens, heading west.

1.7 Reach the intersection where Henry Hollow Loop meets the Ridgetop Trail. **(Option:** The hike can be extended by taking the Ridgetop Trail out and back for an additional 3.4 miles.) Turn right at the intersection, heading north for a short distance and then bearing east. The trail is marked with white and red blazes.

1.9 Pass a path on the left that leads to the Highland Trailhead and shelter. Continue following the trail, which is marked with white blazes, as it weaves through the woods, generally heading north, for about 1 mile with no landmarks, junctions, or paths intersecting it.

2.9 Reach a Y; take the left branch and backtrack to the trailhead.

3.0 End the hike at the trailhead.

Bells Bend: Poplar Hollow Trail

This is a great hike for bird-watchers and sun lovers. The trail is unique in that the surface is a mowed path, about 15 feet wide. You wind through large meadows and woods and nearly reach the Cumberland River, but it stays out of view. Bluebirds and red-winged blackbirds are common. Take time to visit the nature center, which features some excellent exhibits.

Start: Poplar Hollow Trail trailhead adjacent to the parking area
Distance: 2.1-mile lollipop, with an out and back to the nature center
Approximate hiking time: 1.5 hours
Difficulty: Moderate due to no shade
Trail surface: Gravel, grass
Best season: September to June
Other trail users: Dog walkers
Canine compatibility: Leashed dogs permitted
Fees and permits: None required
Schedule: Dawn to dusk
Maps: USGS: Scottsboro; trail maps available at nature center; map board at trailhead kiosk
Trail contact: Nashville Metropolitan Board of Parks and Recreation, P.O. Box 196340, Nashville, TN 37219; (615) 862-8400; www .greenwaysfornashville.org
Other: A porta-potty is located by the parking area. Restrooms and water fountain available at the Nature Center. There is no potable water or restrooms on the trail. Most of the trail has no tree cover to furnish shade. Take adequate water and use sunscreen and insect repellant. The nature center is not always open; call ahead for hours.

Finding the trailhead: From the southwest side of Nashville, take I-40 West toward Memphis and go 3.7 miles. Merge onto Briley Parkway via exit 204A and go 5.1 miles. Take TN 12 North, exit 24, toward Ashland City for 0.2 mile, then turn left onto Hydes Ferry Pike and go 2.9 miles. Turn left onto Old Hickory Boulevard and go 4.8 miles to 4107 Old Hickory Blvd. Follow the park road to the parking area and trailhead. *DeLorme Tennessee Atlas & Gazetteer:* Page 53, B4. GPS: N36 09.36' / W86 55.57'

THE HIKE

Bells Bend opened in 2007, making it one of Nashville's newest parks. Its 800 acres of meadows and scattered woods is bordered on the southwest by the Cumberland River. The corridor between Bells Bend and Beaman Park has maintained its rural landscape, providing a peaceful drive to the park. Bird-watchers will enjoy the open meadows adjoining the isolated woods, which furnish good habitat for many avian species.

This hike forms a clockwise loop with a short out and back to the nature center, where trail maps are available. A kiosk at the trailhead also contains a large map and some information about the park. This trail is underutilized, so those who enjoy hiking in solitude will be pleased.

Heading south from Poplar Hollow Trail trailhead adjacent to the parking area, you immediately cross a bridge over a small creek and continue south on crushed gravel. In a very short distance the trail surface turns to mowed grass, about 4 feet wide. Birds can already be heard, if not seen. Bear slightly to the right and pass a barn on the right used for storing park materials. There is a small wooded picnic area, including picnic tables and grills, behind the barn. The trail flattens a bit and then heads slightly down. Reach an intersection and turn left on the trail heading east toward the nature center. Continue east up a slight hill, with the nature center in sight.

A sister and brother hiking team rest near Bells Bend Park to familiarize themselves with the trail.

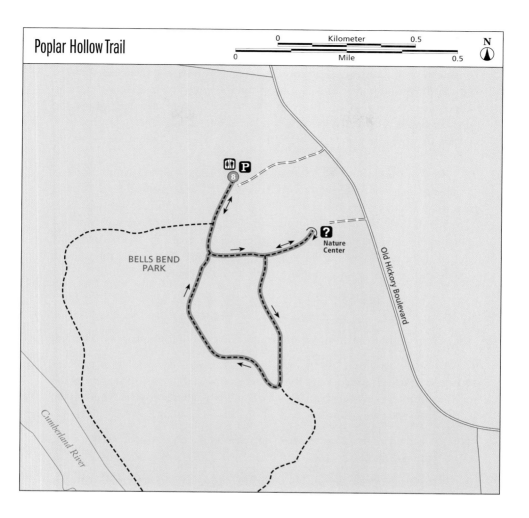

The area on the right and left is a meadow containing a mixture of tall wild-flowers, prairie grass, and weeds. Look for sparrows, including Henslow's sparrow, and blue grosbeaks precariously perched on the sturdier weed stems. Pass a trail intersection and continue heading east to the nature center, and go through the gate to the center's grounds. In the spring and early summer, a multitude of birds can be seen here, including indigo buntings and bluebirds. These are two of the most beautifully colored birds to be found anywhere. The areas in front of and behind the center are mowed and have several benches. Take some time to talk to the ranger and investigate the excellent exhibits in the center. Leave the nature center and at the first trail intersection, turn left, heading south.

At times the mowed trail is 12 feet wide. In the spring butterflies are attracted to some of the wildflowers. The meadow is punctuated by small groups of trees, furnishing shelter for birds and mammals. Also in the spring watch for nesting grassland birds, including the willow flycatcher, dickcissel, and grosbeak. Wild turkeys and bobwhites may be seen throughout the year. A covey of bobwhites taking off can startle even the seasoned hiker. Fencerows are favorite spots for the orchard oriole, red-winged blackbird, indigo bunting, and American woodcock. Follow the trail as it wanders a bit to the right and left and slightly up, heading south.

Reach a Y and take the right branch, which heads slightly down to the west. The left branch heads up and then down, closer to the Cumberland River. The trail is surrounded by weedy meadows, with the tree line along the Cumberland about 300 feet to the west. The wildflowers and weeds reach heights of 4 feet. Make a hard right as the trail heads north and follows along small hills and flatlands. The nature center can be seen to the right, over the meadow. Reach a trail intersection that leads to the center and continue north, backtracking to the trailhead.

MILES AND DIRECTIONS

0.0 Start at the Poplar Hollow Trail trailhead adjacent to the parking area and head south across a bridge.

0.1 The trail surface changes from gravel to mowed grass. To the right of the trail is a park storage barn. A picnic area, with tables and grills, is behind the barn in a wooded area.

0.3 Reach an intersection and turn left, going up a slight rise east toward the nature center.

0.4 Cross an intersection and continue heading east toward the nature center.

0.6 Reach the nature center. Get map and then backtrack to the first intersection.

0.9 At the intersection, turn left and head south.

1.2 Follow the trail as it zigzags a little until reaching a Y. Take the right branch as it heads slightly down and west. The Cumberland River is on the left, but cannot be seen.

1.5 The mowed trail meanders with some minor ups and downs. Follow the trail as it makes a hard right, heading north.

1.7 The nature center can be seen in the distance to the right. Continue following the trail until reaching an intersection. The right trail (which had previously been followed) leads to the nature center. Continue going straight ahead (north) toward the trailhead. Pass the barn and picnic grounds on the left.

2.1 End the hike at the trailhead.

Percy Priest Lake: Three Hickories Trail

This is an excellent hike for families with young children. The interpretive brochure explains a number of sites on the trail that takes you through the woods and karst topography, with its limestone outcrops and sinkholes. Along the shoreline of the lake, watch for turtles, waterbirds, and lake insects. This area also contains cedar glades, with their rare plants. Enjoy Mother Nature at her best!

Start: Three Hickories Trail trailhead adjacent to the parking area
Distance: 1.3-mile counterclockwise loop
Approximate hiking time: 1 hour
Difficulty: Easy due to flat shaded trail
Trail surface: Dirt, rock
Best season: Year-round
Other trail users: Dog walkers
Canine compatibility: Leashed dogs permitted
Fees and permits: None required
Schedule: Dawn to 8:00 p.m. (gates are locked at 8:00 p.m.)

Maps: USGS: Hermitage; trail maps and interpretive guides available at park headquarters
Trail contact: U.S. Army Corps of Engineers, 3737 Bell Rd., Nashville, TN 37214-2660; (615) 889-1975; www.recreation.gov
Other: Bicycles are not allowed on the trail. Water fountains and restrooms are available in the campground adjoining the parking area. There is no potable water or restrooms on the trail. Take adequate drinking water, and use sunscreen and insect repellant.

Finding the trailhead: From downtown Nashville, take I-40 East 7 miles to exit 221B. Turn right on Old Hickory Boulevard and then left on Bell Road (there are Corps directional signs from this point on). Turn right on New Hope Road and go 1 mile, then turn right on Stewarts Ferry Pike and left on Old Hickory Boulevard for 1 mile to the Cook Recreation Area. The parking area is adjacent to the lake and campground area. The trail entrance is across from the amphitheater in the day-use area. *DeLorme Tennessee Atlas & Gazetteer:* Page 53, D7. GPS: N36 08.15' / W86 36.12'

This is karst and cedar glade country. A karst is an area with little to no topsoil, with limestone outcrops reaching to the surface. The underlayer of limestone is gradually dissolved by water seeping through, allowing caves, passageways, and underground streams to be formed. This underground world has its own unique flora and fauna. Over time the top layers of limestone over the caves collapse, forming sinkholes and crevasses, which are the signature features of a karst. Cedar glades are also associated with karst areas. The glades are thick stands of usually red cedar trees that surround a limestone-surfaced, gravel-strewn meadow. Middle Tennessee has some of the largest karst and cedar glade areas in the country.

Before your hike, stop at the ranger post located at the entrance and ask for a trail map and interpretive guide. Drive to the large paved parking area adjacent to the lake. A great view of the lake is available from the parking area. Start at the Three Hickories Trail trailhead at the edge of the paved parking area and immediately go into the cedar woods, heading east and then south to a short connector trail to a Y, where the loop starts. Take the right branch and follow in a counterclockwise direction to keep the interpretive stations in sequence. (One loop was

This sinkhole is just one of several on the Three Hickories Trail. Use caution when approaching any sinkhole.

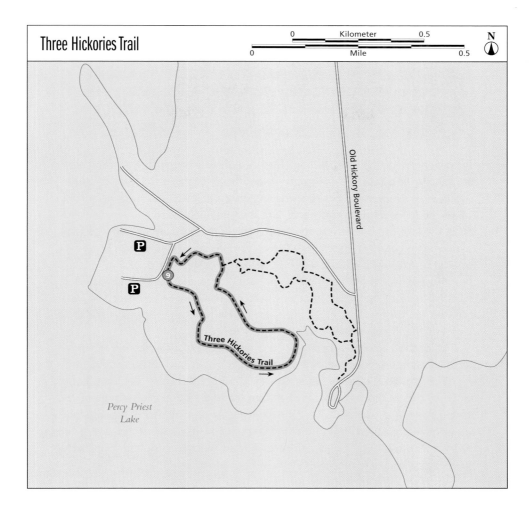

0   Kilometer   0.5

0   Mile   0.5

N

Old Hickory Boulevard

Three Hickories Trail

Percy Priest Lake

chosen for this hike among the several on the trail; therefore, not all the interpretive stations will be seen. Use the trail map to locate the other loops.)

Follow the trail as it narrows, sometimes down to only 12 to 15 inches wide. Zigzag and weave through the woods and continue generally south, passing Interpretive Station 2 on the left. Notice the large number of hickory trees in the woods—the trail could have been named the Three Hundred Hickories Trail! In the fall hundreds of hickory nuts fall to the ground. They are good to eat, but very difficult to shell. Take a small bag of them home and experiment. Reach a section of fence surrounding a large sinkhole and crevasse. Horizontal layers of limestone can be seen along the sides of the sinkhole. The Shawnee Indians called these *bein-shawee,* meaning "deep water." A few locals have adopted this term, but pronounce it *boomshaw.* Take a hard left around the fence, heading generally south.

9

Bear right and left, with bushes and trees along the edge of the trail, and break into an area with little tree canopy. The woods have changed from cedar to hardwoods, mostly hickories. Continue weaving back and forth until reaching a fence. Follow the fence for a short distance and then bear left, heading away from the fence. The lake can be seen through the trees on the right, about 300 feet away. Take a hard left and temporarily head away from the lake. The trail then bears back toward the lake, while passing Interpretive Station 6. This is an easy spot to take a short out and back to the lakeshore. Look around for animal and bird tracks, including mink, muskrat, opossum, great blue heron, Canada goose, and coot. The water level can vary, depending on releases from the dam. Return to the trail and head north and then west, bearing away from the lake.

Notice the numerous limestone outcrops in the woods and encroaching on the trail. Pass Interpretive Station 8 on the right and bear hard right, heading northwest. This is good habitat for birds, with each species having its own niche determined by the location of food. Towhees are seed eaters and can be seen on the ground, while flycatchers stay near the treetops, looking for insects. Woodpeckers can be heard and seen on the trunks of trees. Cardinals frequent this area, using the bark of cedar trees to build their nests. Add an extra dimension to your hike by carrying a bird guide to help identify the various species.

Reach a Y and take the left branch. Pass a blue blaze and take a hard left, heading west to the end of the hike at the trailhead.

MILES AND DIRECTIONS

0.0 Start at the Three Hickories Trail trailhead at the edge of the paved parking area. Head east, passing Interpretive Station 1 at the trailhead. The trail is identified with blue blazes on trees.

0.1 Within 100 feet of the trailhead, reach a Y and take the right branch, heading southeast, then bear right, heading south (this will keep the trail signs relating to the interpretive guide in sequence). Pass Interpretive Station 2.

0.2 Continue following the trail around a fence protecting a large sinkhole and bear left, heading southeast. Pass Interpretive Stations 3 and 4 and continue following the trail southeast. **Note:** Even though the trail is a counterclockwise loop, it zigs, zags, and may even double back on itself, so that at any time the hike description, miles and directions, or map could go in an opposite direction for a short distance.

0.4 Follow the trail as it leads toward a boundary fence, then follow along the fence line, heading north. Bear left, going away from the fence, and pass Interpretive Station 5. Percy Priest Lake can be seen on the right. Bear hard left, heading west away from the lake, and then right toward the shore.

0.6 Make your own short out and back through the trees, to the edge of the lake. Return to the trail and bear slightly left. Continue heading west, away from the lake. Follow the trail as it enters the woods and squiggles right, left, and right again, heading generally northwest through limestone outcrops.

0.9 Continue following the trail generally northwest as it weaves around limestone outcrops and goes up and down minor slopes. Go up four limestone "steps" and continue following the trail as it heads northwest. This is the most strenuous section of the hike.

1.0 Reach a Y and take the left branch, heading west toward Interpretive Station 16 and the trailhead.

1.1 Pass Interpretive Station 16 on the right and bear hard left, heading west by northwest. The trail is straight and flat as it heads southwest toward the trailhead.

1.3 End the hike at the trailhead.

> *The community of Jefferson was demolished in the early 1960s for the building of the Percy Priest Lake Dam. The town site was inundated by the reservoir. J. Percy Priest Lake was one of the first Corps of Engineers reservoirs to include recreation as part of its justification for being built.*

Long Hunter State Park: Couchville Lake Trail

Lake, woods, and tree lovers will appreciate the new Couchville Lake Arboretum, which borders the trail. Deer and waterbirds are easy to see while following the trail as it does an easy loop around the lake. A 300-foot wooden bridge crosses the lake and affords great photo ops. Many short out-and-back paths lead to the lake's edge and several ponds that border the trail.

Start: Couchville Lake Trail trailhead adjacent to the boathouse
Distance: 2.1-mile clockwise loop
Approximate hiking time: 1.5 hours to allow time to read interpretive information
Difficulty: Easy due to flat paved trail
Trail surface: Asphalt
Best season: Year-round
Other trail users: Bird-watchers, wheelchairs, strollers
Canine compatibility: Dogs not permitted

Fees and permits: None required
Schedule: 7:00 a.m. to sunset
Maps: USGS: LaVergne; trail maps and interpretive guides available at park office
Trail contact: Long Hunter State Park, 2910 Hobson Pike, Hermitage, TN 37076; (615) 885-2422; www.state.tn.us/environment /parks
Other: Water and restrooms are available at the park office and boathouse. There is no potable water or restrooms on the trail.

Finding the trailhead: From the east side of Nashville, take I-40 East to Mount Juliet Road, exit 226A. Go south (right) 6.2 miles to the main park entrance and proceed to the headquarters. *DeLorme Tennessee Atlas & Gazetteer:* Page 53, D7. GPS: N36 05.67' / W86 32.66'

Couchville Lake was formed in 1968 when Percy Priest Lake was created. The Couchville Lake Arboretum that borders the trail was the first certified arboretum in a Tennessee state park. This 2,800-acre park with more than 17 miles of trails, ranging from less than a mile to 6 miles, may offer hikers the best combination of hikes near Nashville. Long Hunter State Park took its name from early explorers who were called "long hunters" due to the time they spent in the field. The Stones River, which feeds the 14,000-acre Percy Priest Reservoir, runs through this area. In the 1700s this was choice hunting grounds for Native Americans, including Shawnee, Choctaw, Cherokee, and Chickasaw. Their battles with incoming settlers were fierce, leading to naming one of the trails to Nashville the War Trace.

Pick up a trail map and interpretive brochure at the park headquarters and drive the short distance to the boathouse parking area. The hike starts at the Couchville Lake Trail trailhead adjacent to the boathouse. Benches are placed conveniently around the loop. Hiking in the late afternoon affords the opportunity to see the sunset across the lake, an inspiring sight.

Follow the loop in a clockwise direction, heading generally north, with the lake on the right and woods on the left. Pass the first of several concrete or gravel paths

Couchville Lake was created when Percy Priest Reservoir was developed. The paved trail around the lake is also an arboretum.

that lead to fishing platforms, and watch for leaf patterns painted on the trail surface. These relate to the Arboretum Interpretive Guide which describes the trees. The trees are also identified by nameplates about 7 feet up their trunks. The first tree in the guide is a shagbark hickory. The trail also has general information signs, such as one on wild turkeys.

Keep alert for wild animals, especially deer feeding in the woods. Early morning and late afternoon afford the best opportunities for viewing. In about 1,000 feet, reach a gravel path that leads to the lake—take the opportunity to go to the edge and investigate the water world. Depending on the season, bullfrogs, turtles, dragonflies, minnows, mayflies, water snakes, and various other water-dwelling creatures may be seen. Continue following the loop as the lake comes in and out of view, depending on the tree cover. Even though the trail is shown as a near-perfect loop on the map, it zigs and zags, so that at any time the hike could go in an opposite direction for a short distance.

Follow the trail as it bears generally right to a bridge crossing the north part of the lake. The 300-foot bridge affords great photo ops. The boathouse can be seen, along with some high-tension wires. After crossing the bridge make a hard right, with the lake on the right and heavy woods containing black willow and white and black oak, on both sides of the trail. Watch for poison ivy, with its telltale three leaves—it may take the form of groundcover or climb on trees. Pass a small seasonal pond on the left about 10 feet away, and look for animal tracks leading to the pond.

At about 1 mile you reach a small A-frame shelter. The shelter has benches and is a good place to sit and look around for a few minutes. Make a hard right after the shelter and break into a patch of open canopy. Watch for limestone outcrops and one section that is flat and resembles a sidewalk. The trail squiggles back and forth a bit and passes some paths to fishing platforms. This area contains a large number of limestone outcrops and rocks. Use the interpretive guide to garner information about the trees in the arboretum.

Continue straight and then hard right around the end of the lake, which is barely visible through the heavy woods. Pass two small seasonal ponds on the left, with a path leading to them. Look for a limestone "wall" over 4 feet high about 20 feet away. At the end of the wall, bear hard right and then left past a bench. Pass the arboretum sign for chinkapin oak and Virginia creeper to end the hike.

MILES AND DIRECTIONS

0.0 Start at the Couchville Lake Trail trailhead across the parking area, at the boathouse. Watch for the information signs for this self-guided nature/arboretum trail.

0.1 Pass several information signs identifying trees. Couchville Lake can be seen through the trees to the right.

Couchville Lake Trail

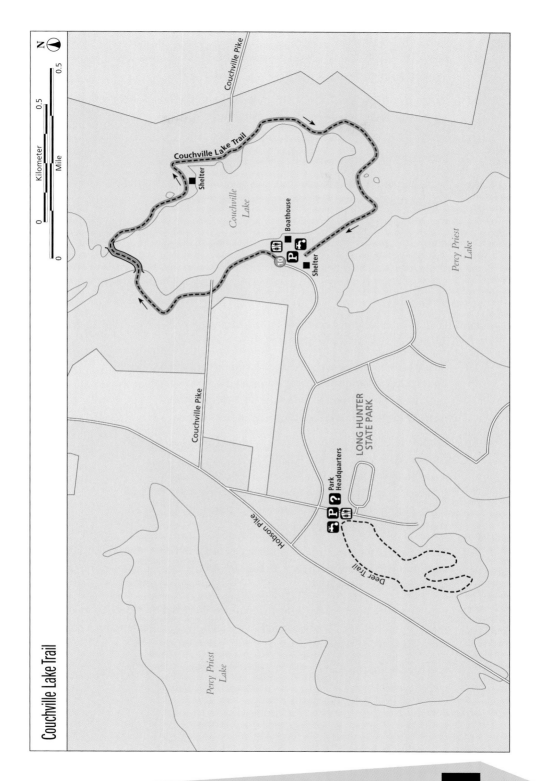

0.2 Follow the asphalt trail, passing several arboretum information signs. Pass a gravel path to the right that leads to the lake.

0.3 Pass a wood bench overlooking the lake. From the bench bear left, then right, continuing in a generally northwest direction.

0.4 Arrive at another bench and take a hard right. Follow the trail across the 300-foot-long bridge across the lake.

0.6 Bend hard right, heading southeast while following along the edge of the lake. Continue to pass arboretum information signs.

0.7 Pass a bench and follow the trail along the lake edge, while passing arboretum information signs. The lake is on the right, about 45 feet away.

0.8 Follow the trail as it bends left and right between the trees. Pass a bench and bear slightly left. This leg of the loop heads generally in a southeasterly direction.

0.9 Pass a seasonal pond on the left. The lake is on the right, about 15 feet away. Continue following the trail along the lake edge.

1.0 Reach a small A-frame shelter that has benches and a trash barrel. After visiting the shelter, return to the trail. Follow the trail a short distance and make a hard right, then head southeast toward the south end of the lake.

1.2 Continue following the trail past a bench and arboretum information signs. The trail zigzags as it generally follows the lake edge to the right. Pass a gravel path to a fishing pier about 35 feet to the right. The trail bears slightly to the left and then weaves right and left, generally following the lake edge in a southerly direction.

1.5 Pass several arboretum information signs and a bench as the trails tracks right and left. Follow the trail, with the lake on the right. Circle around the southern edge of the lake.

1.8 A path on the right leads to the lake; take a short out and back to investigate the shoreline. Pass two small seasonal ponds on the left and a concrete sidewalk on the right that leads to a fishing pier.

2.1 End the hike at the trail's end, adjoining the parking area.

The 1,000-Year Flood

On Saturday night, on the first of May 2010, it started to rain—at first a gentle rain that most of the residents of Nashville and the surrounding area welcomed. Then a strong weather system changed the gentle rain into a severe storm with torrential downpours. By Sunday, the storm had already inundated some sections in and around Nashville with 19 inches of rain. Parts of I-40 were under 20 feet of water—a mobile home was photographed floating along the highway on Monday. Sections of both I-40 and I-65 were closed. The boundary of a frontal system had stalled over Nashville. This, coupled with very moist air flowing northward from the Gulf of Mexico, set the stage for the heavy rain to continue into Monday.

This rainfall also made May 2010 the wettest May on record. The previous record of 11.84 inches had been established in May 1983. The Cumberland River crested in Nashville at 51.86 feet at 6:00 p.m. CST. A level this high had not been recorded since 1937, which was prior to the flood-control systems put in place by the U.S. Army Corps of Engineers. The all-time record set in 1937 is 53.9 feet; the flood stage is 40 feet. Record river crests were also seen in Clarksville (hikes 35 and 36). The Couchville Lake Trail (hike 10) and the Three Hickories Trail (hike 9) in Long Hunter State Park in Hermitage and adjoining Percy Priest Lake recorded over 20 feet of water. Three weeks after the flood there was still 5 feet of water covering the Couchville Lake Trail. Carnton Road, leading to the Carnton Plantation and hike 18, was covered with 5 feet of water. All of the greenway trails in Murfreesboro (hikes 25 to 30) were flooded, and trails in Brentwood bordering the Little Harpeth River recorded more than 15 feet. Much of the trail around the bend of the Harpeth was destroyed and had to be deleted from this guide.

The Cumberland River damaged the Grand Ole Opry House and much around it, but the Ryman Opry House, home of the original Grand Ole Opry for years, was spared. The common areas of the Gaylord Opryland Hotel were destroyed, and some parts of the hotel were under 10 feet of water. The playing fields for the Tennessee Titans, Nashville's NFL team, and the indoor arena used by the Nashville Predators, its NHL team, were covered by several feet of water.

On May 4 Nashville/Davidson County was declared a Federal Disaster Area. Preliminary damage estimates were placed at $1.9 billion. Working side by side, 1,533 volunteers logged 63,285 work hours between May 2 and May 23. Ten deaths were recorded in Davidson County, which includes Nashville. May 2010 will go down in history as the month of the 1,000-Year Flood. Those who lived here at the time will be able to tell some historic tales to their grandchildren.

Long Hunter State Park: Deer Trail

This is a great hike for deer lovers and lake lovers. The flat trail winds through the woods and then follows the edge of Percy Priest Lake. Great views are available of the lake and its shore. Explore the beach, which is littered with shells and driftwood, and watch in the nearby woods for deer trails and the deer themselves. Birds are especially numerous during the spring.

Start: Deer Trail trailhead adjacent to the park headquarters parking area

Distance: 1.2-mile counterclockwise loop

Approximate hiking time: 1 hour

Difficulty: Easy due to flat shaded trail

Trail surface: Dirt

Best season: Year-round

Other trail users: Bird-watchers, dog walkers

Canine compatibility: Leashed dogs permitted

Fees and permits: None required

Schedule: 7:00 a.m. to sunset

Maps: USGS: LaVergne; trail maps and interpretive guides available at park office

Trail contact: Long Hunter State Park, 2910 Hobson Pike, Hermitage, TN 37076; (615) 885-2422; www.state.tn.us/environment /parks

Other: Water and restrooms are available at the park office and boathouse. There is no potable water or restrooms on the trail. Take adequate water, as this hike can be humid. Be sure to use insect repellant, for many deer ticks call this trail home, and their bites can cause Lyme disease. During and after the hike, check your body and clothing for these hitchhikers.

Finding the trailhead: From the east side of Nashville, take I-40 East to Mount Juliet Road, exit 226A. Go south (right) 6.2 miles to the main park entrance and proceed to the park headquarters. *DeLorme Tennessee Atlas & Gazetteer:* Page 53, D7. GPS: N36 05.67' / W86 32.66'

Pick up a trail map at the park headquarters before your hike, which follows a loop counterclockwise as it wanders right and left and follows a portion of Percy Priest Lake. Start at the Deer Trail trailhead adjacent to the park headquarters, and head west on a short connector trail. Almost immediately you reach a Y; take the right branch, bearing left and heading generally southwest. The trail is about 3 feet wide, with tall grass, bushes, cedars, and hardwood trees along both edges. The tree canopy is intermittent, sometimes furnishing good shade and other times none.

Bear hard right at an information sign describing animal tracks, still generally heading south. Notice the several brush piles that have been constructed by park rangers. These will furnish cover for birds, small mammals, spiders, beetles, and all sorts of other critters. Pass another information sign on the right, telling about sumac. While continuing to head south, notice the large number of moss plants scattered through the woods. The trail is basically flat, with some minor grades up and down. The woods change to mixed cedar and hardwoods, including oak and hickory trees. In the fall hickory nuts can be seen on the trail and in the woods. The nuts are pear-shaped, about 1 to 1½ inches long. Pass a sign on the right with information about sassafras. In the spring bees use sassafras nectar to fill their honeycombs, and in the fall birds enjoy the tree's blue-black berries.

A portion of Percy Priest Lake can be seen to the right through the trees and down a slope. A narrow path intersects from the right, while the trail bears left. Follow the path for a short out and back to the lakeshore, passing some limestone outcrops on the way to the lake. Once at the shore, two different views are available. The left view contains the lakeshore, rocks, and the woods, while the

Dear Trail in Long Hunter State Park leads to the edge of Percy Priest Reservoir. The bridge over the reservoir and high-tension transmission towers may be seen.

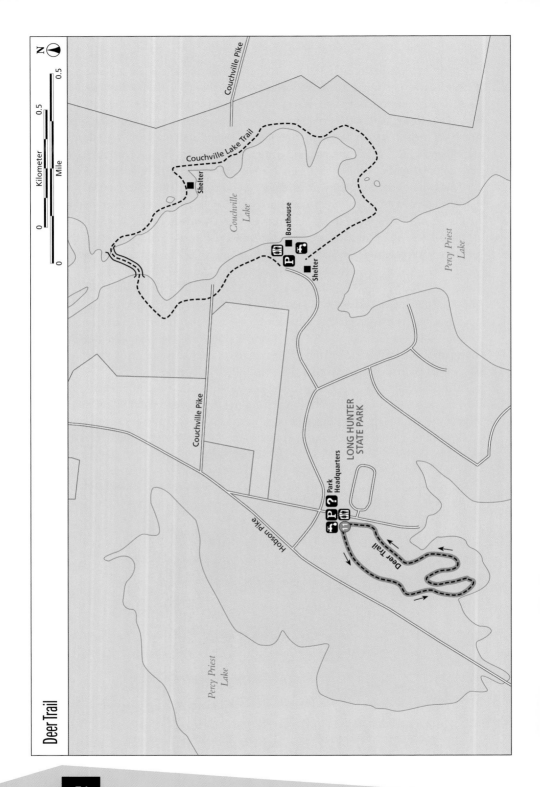

Deer Trail

right view shows a bridge and power lines. The water is shallow and clear at the lake's edge. Look for water creatures and small shells, and keep an eye out for fish jumping in the water. After kicking back and enjoying the solitude and scenery, return to the Deer Trail, heading north.

Bear right, then left in a tight semicircle. Deer paths cross the trail leading in and out of the woods. The does give birth to their fawns in the spring, and this time of the year furnishes some great photo ops. The fall is also a good time to witness deer activity. The bucks, recognized by their antlers, are in rut and eager to mate, and are less cautious than normal. Early morning and late afternoon afford the best chance to see deer. The woods contain mostly cedar trees, mixed with oaks and maples. Pass an information sign explaining decomposers, which are part of nature's recycling system and include bacteria, fungi, and insects. Reach a Y and take the right branch, which is the short connector trail back to the trailhead.

MILES AND DIRECTIONS

0.0 Start at the Deer Trail trailhead adjacent to the headquarters parking area and head west, then southwest.

0.1 Follow a 150-foot connector to a Y. Take the right branch and bear left, heading southwest. Pass an information sign about animal tracks and bear hard right, then left in a short semicircle as the trail weaves through the trees, heading generally southwest.

0.4 Take a hard left, almost doubling back on the trail, then take a hard right and go down a slope, passing an information sign about sassafras, still heading generally southwest. **(Note:** While the trail is a counterclockwise loop, it zigs, zags, and even doubles back on itself, so that at any time the hike description, miles and directions, or map could go in an opposite direction for a short distance.)

0.6 Reach a path that intersects from the right. Follow the path for a short out and back to the shore of Percy Priest Lake. Return to the Deer Trail and turn right. Follow the trail as it veers right, left, and back right, still heading generally north.

0.9 Reach an information sign about decomposers. Bear left at the sign and follow the trail as it squiggles through the woods, still generally heading north.

1.1 Follow the trail as the surface changes to flat limestone. Reach a Y and take the right branch, which is the short connector back to the trailhead. Backtrack to the trailhead.

1.2 End the hike at the trailhead.

Long Hunter State Park: Jones Mill Mountain Bike Trail

Follow the single-track mountain bike trail through cedar glades and hardwood forest, near the shores of Percy Priest Lake. The predominantly oak and hickory forests are home to many birds, including hawks. Watch for birds on the ground and flying in and out of the woods. The reservoir can be seen through the trees. In the spring notice the variety of mosses along the trail.

Start: Jones Mill Mountain Bike Trail trailhead adjacent to the parking area

Distance: 2.0-mile clockwise loop

Approximate hiking time: 1.5 hours

Difficulty: Moderate due to narrow trails and elevation change

Trail surface: Dirt, limestone, gravel

Best season: Year-round

Other trail users: Mountain bikers, bird-watchers

Canine compatibility: Leashed dogs permitted

Fees and permits: None required

Schedule: 7:00 a.m. to sunset

Maps: USGS: LaVergne

Trail contact: Long Hunter State Park, 2910 Hobson Pike, Hermitage, TN 37076; (615) 885-2422; www.state.tn.us/environment/parks

Other: Water and restrooms are available at the park office and boathouse. There is no potable water or restrooms on the trail. Tree cover furnishing shade is intermittent. Take adequate water, wear a hat, and use sunscreen and insect repellant. Sturdy shoes are recommended due to the many stretches of rocky surface.

Finding the trailhead: From the east side of Nashville, take I-40 East to Mount Juliet Road, exit 226A. Go south (right) 6.2 miles and pass the park entrance, then follow Mount Juliet Road northeast for 5 miles to reach the parking area at the Jones Mill Mountain Bike Trail. *DeLorme Tennessee Atlas & Gazetteer:* Page 53, D7. GPS: N36 04.48' / W86 30.58'

Thise trail was designed by mountain bikers as a single-track workout. It passes through dense woods and open cedar glades and around limestone outcrops. Blue blazes on trees identify the route. Although mountain bikers utilize the trail mostly on weekends, be alert at all times, for the trail is narrow and hilly and wanders to the right and left, limiting vision. Stay as far to the right as possible, and move off the trail when a biker approaches.

The clockwise loop follows the hilly terrain up and down and weaves back and forth. Bird-watchers will appreciate the number of species, including hawks and owls, that may be seen. Hikers interested in geology will have a field day.

Start at the Jones Mill Mountain Bike Trail trailhead and kiosk adjacent to the parking area and head south into the woods. The trail surface starts out as crushed gravel but quickly changes to dirt and limestone. Almost immediately reach a Y and take the left branch. The woods on each side of the trail are deep, and the songs of a variety of birds may be heard. Follow the trail as it heads slightly up and veers right, left, and back right, heading generally south. Specific compass directions are nearly useless, since the trail rarely tracks in a single direction for more than 20 yards. This makes the hike more interesting by creating anticipation of the unknown at each turn.

In the spring the woods and open areas are filled with wildflowers. Pass a small clearing containing several limestone outcrops. For those interested in geology, this is karst territory, but it lacks the numerous sinkholes and crevasses found in

Jones Mill Mountain Bike Trail in Long Hunter State Park leads through dense wood, but also over flat outcrops of limestone.

other areas in middle Tennessee. A karst has little or no soil on the surface and is underlaid with limestone. Rain and groundwater seeping through the surface eventually erodes the limestone, creating caves, sinkholes, and underground streams. Karsts have their own distinct species of flora and fauna.

In the spring it's possible to see a variety of butterflies, which is good, and swarms of mosquitoes, which is not so good. Watch for birds in the woods, including cardinals and sometimes hawks. It's interesting to observe hawks flying between the trees at relatively high speeds. Watch your footing, because tree roots and loose rocks sometimes clutter the surface. Break into a cedar glade area with no shade, and look for pale blue glade phlox, which carpets the rocky outcrops, and Tennessee milk vetch displaying their pale yellow flowers.

Follow a semicircle left and pass a small meadow containing young cedar trees. In the spring this area is ablaze with wildflowers. The trail surface changes to mostly gravel and back again to dirt. Look for clumps of moss in the woods, including Christmas moss, which is grayish green and grows less than a foot high and a foot in diameter. Weave right and left until reaching a Y, and take the right branch. This is a shortcut to return to the main loop and trailhead. Those desiring to extend their hike can take the left branch to Bald Knob, adding more than 2 miles.

At about 1.2 miles reach a T and take the right branch. Pass an area on the left covered with large limestone outcrops. Continue following the trail as it zigzags and follows the terrain up and down. Pass a grassy meadow about 50 feet deep and 300 feet long. At about 1.8 miles glimpses of Percy Priest Lake are visible to the left. Watch for small lizards as they dart across the trail. A walk over some large, flat sections of limestone takes you back to the trailhead.

MILES AND DIRECTIONS

0.0 Start at the Jones Mill Mountain Bike Trail trailhead adjacent to the parking area. The trail is identified by blue blazes on trees.

0.1 In less than 100 feet, reach a Y and take the left branch. Continue following the trail marked by blue blazes.

0.3 Pass a clearing and flat limestone outcrop to the right. Continue following the blue-blazed trail, which becomes rocky.

0.5 Reach a blue-blazed tree on the left and bear right.

0.7 Reach a small clearing covered by flat limestone. Bear left and then right, as the trail forms a small semicircle.

1.0 Follow the trail as it bears right, left and right again through the woods. Reach a Y and take the right branch, which is a shortcut to the trailhead. The left branch continues to Bald Knob and would add more than 2 miles to the hike.

Jones Mill Mountain Bike Trail

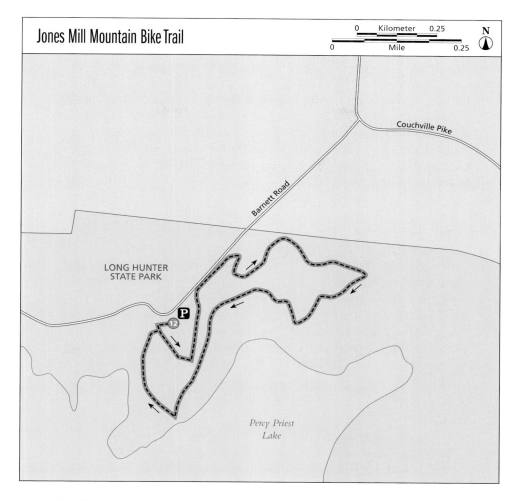

1.2 The trail narrows and heads slightly down while weaving between the trees. Pass a large cedar that splits into two trunks. Bear left and then right and reach a T. Take the right branch back toward the trailhead.

1.3 Pass a large clearing on the left filled with flat limestone outcrops covering an area about 50 feet wide and 120 feet deep. Follow the blue blazes as the trail wanders right and left.

1.5 Continue following the blue blazes as the trail veers right and left. Pass a grassy meadow on the left, about 50 feet deep and 300 feet long.

1.8 Follow the trail slightly up, with woods on the right and left. Percy Priest Lake can be seen down a slope, through the trees, about 400 feet away. Continue following the blue blazes, heading toward the trailhead.

2.0 End the hike at the trailhead.

Couchville Cedar Glade State Natural Area: Tyler Alley Sykes Trail

This hike will especially appeal to those who enjoy the rare flowers and other plant life found only in cedar glades. The trail passes through small woodland patches and into the barrens, followed by a solid limestone surface leading to a bridge and a small seasonal pool. This is typical karst topography. After a heavy rain, this normally dry and barren area can produce temporary streamlets, allowing a few amphibians, including frogs, to survive.

Start: Tyler Alley Sykes Trail trail-head adjacent to the parking area
Distance: 1.2-mile lollipop
Approximate hiking time: 1 hour
Difficulty: Easy due to flat trail
Trail surface: Dirt, grass, rock
Best season: September to June
Other trail users: Dog walkers
Canine compatibility: Leashed dogs permitted
Fees and permits: None required

Schedule: Dawn to dusk
Maps: USGS: LaVergne
Trail contact: Long Hunter State Park, 2910 Hobson Pike, Hermitage, TN 37076; (615) 885-2422; www.tennessee.gov/environ ment/nh
Other: There is no potable water or restrooms on the trail. Take adequate water, use insect repellant, and wear a hat.

Finding the trailhead: From the east side of Nashville, take I-40 East to Mount Juliet Road, exit 226A. Go south (right) 6.2 miles, pass the main park entrance, and continue south on South Mount Juliet Road for about 6 miles to reach the parking area on the right. *DeLorme Tennessee Atlas & Gazetteer:* Page 53, D7. GPS: N36 06 08' / W86 31.77'

This trail is located in the Couchville Cedar Glade, a 122-acre state natural area in the Nashville central basin. The glade is contiguous to the east boundary of Long Hunter State Park and was acquired by the state from the Nature Conservancy in 1995. The trail was named in honor of Tyler Alley Sykes, a dedicated young biologist, wife, and mother who unexpectedly passed away at the age of thirty-one. She played a critical role in working with the state on a federal grant from the U.S. Fish and Wildlife Service to acquire twenty-five acres to protect the remainder of the Tennessee coneflower population, which was outside of the natural area's boundaries.

The Couchville Cedar Glade is noted for sheltering the largest and best-quality Tennessee coneflowers, an endangered species. The trail leads through an area where the glades and barrens interface, creating one of the finest examples of a glades-barrens complex. Hikers interested in karst topography, cedar glades, and rare flowers will especially appreciate this hike. Benches are conveniently placed along the trail. Most of the trail is identified with white blazes, and a portion has marker posts with directional arrows.

Go through the gate adjacent to the small parking area and head west. The trail is about 3 feet wide with a grass and dirt surface. Almost immediately you

The Tyler Alley Sykes Trail passes by an area of flat limestone that, after a heavy rain, may have a small stream unusual in cedar glades.

reach a kiosk on the left that contains a map and short biography of Tyler Alley Sykes. In less than 0.1 mile there is a Y; take the right branch, heading northwest to walk the loop counterclockwise. Follow the flat trail as it veers left and right, and notice the reduced size of the trees, which include cedars and hardwoods. There is virtually no understory beneath the trees.

Pass a bench on the right that faces a barrens. No area could be more aptly named. This is a very difficult environment for flora and fauna, and it is hard to imagine how the pioneers attempted to farm this land. Pass near a fence that protects a ten-acre plot of the endangered Tennessee coneflower. Follow the trail as it makes a hard left away from the fence, still heading generally west by northwest. The trail heads slightly up, and a heavy rain can cause several inches of water to cover it. Follow the trail as it becomes rockier and is crossed by some low limestone outcrops. Single rows of short cedars resemble a line of sentinels.

The tall grasses on both sides of the trail consist of little bluestem and side oats grama. As the trail tracks along the west side of the cedar glades, notice the various stunted shagbark hickories, chinkapin oaks, and white oaks. Some of the woods in this type of karst support moss, sedum, shooting stars, and columbine. In the spring, if the season has been moist, these plants look like a natural rock garden. Many of the plants that live in these cedar glades grow nowhere else in the world. Although areas adjacent to the trail appear rugged, with their limestone outcrops, they are extremely fragile. Tread lightly and try to avoid stepping on the plants.

Continue heading generally southwest, even as the trail veers left, right, and left again. Upon reaching a large section of surface limestone, bear right and take a short out and back to explore a small pond and seasonal stream. The pond's water is about 6 inches deep and crystal clear. This may be the visual highlight of the hike and is the best opportunity for photos. In the spring small tree frogs called spring beepers may be heard. Return to the trail and cross a bridge on the left, then turn left at the end of the bridge, heading southeast. On the right cedar trees are in the majority, while on the left there is a mixture of stunted hardwoods and cedars. Pass 300 to 400 feet of limestone, ringed by cedar trees. This is a really interesting sight.

Pass a bench and cross a bridge over a wet area, then almost immediately cross another bridge over a seasonal stream. There is no tree cover here and the area is mostly grass with large meadow-like areas. Continue heading east while passing near the fence surrounding the ten acres of Tennessee coneflowers. Follow the trail back to the trailhead to end the hike.

MILES AND DIRECTIONS

0.0 Start at the Tyler Alley Sykes Trail trailhead adjacent to the small parking area.

0.1 Enter through the gate and follow the trail slightly left, heading west. In a very short distance, reach a kiosk with a park map and continue following

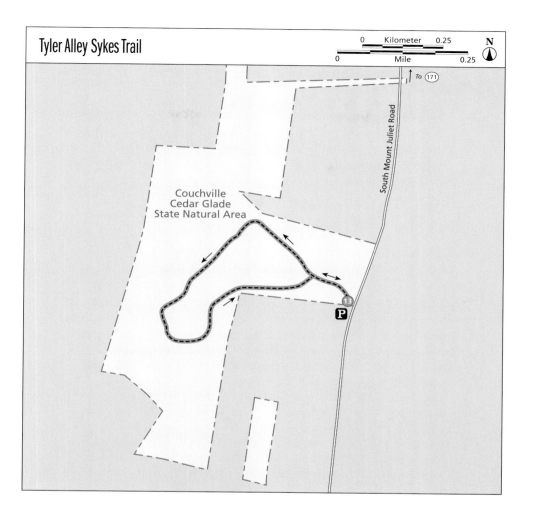

Tyler Alley Sykes Trail

Couchville
Cedar Glade
State Natural Area

South Mount Juliet Road

To 171

0 Kilometer 0.25
0 Mile 0.25
N

the trail west. Reach a Y and take the right branch to investigate the barrens area. This section of the trail is identified by white blazes on trees.

0.3 Follow the trail as it veers right, left, and right again. Take a hard left, going away from the fence protecting the endangered Tennessee coneflowers. Continue following the trail northwest until passing a park bench and bearing southwest.

0.5 Pass a trail marker post on the left and continue following the trail northwest.

0.6 Reach a trail marker post pointing west by southwest. There is a park bench behind the post. Follow the trail as it zigzags around the cedar trees and reaches a small clearing. The trail heads right and in a short distance reaches a bridge over limestone and a wet area. Before crossing the bridge, explore the small seasonal stream and pond. Backtrack to the bridge and cross it, then turn left at the end of the bridge, now heading in a generally southeast direction.

0.9 Follow the trail as it veers right, left, and right again. Pass a large flat section of limestone and bear hard right, heading southeast. Pass a park bench and continue heading southeast, toward the trailhead. Bear left, going through some cedars and heading east, and follow the trail to the fence. Skirt along the fence, following it east to the trailhead.

1.2 End the hike at the trailhead.

Middle Tennessee's Cedar Glades

Middle Tennessee is famous for its cedar glades, and they are particularly interesting to hike through due to their unusual appearance. Cedar glades are a unique type of ecosystem that has adapted to thin or no soil. These areas are usually found where there is karst topography. Karsts are created when falling rain erodes the fairly soluble limestone layer. This creates exposed limestone bedrock, caves, sinkholes, and underground streams.

Couchville Cedar Glade (hike 13), Cedars of Lebanon State Park (hikes 14, 15, and 16) and Vesta Cedar Glade (hike 17) are well known for their glades. The glades resemble a limestone-surfaced, gravel-strewn meadow and are usually surrounded by thick stands of red cedar trees. Most of them include small areas of exposed limestone where nothing grows, gravelly surfaces where sturdy grasses and mosses grow, and a few spots with thin soil surface where small shrubs can survive. In Cedars of Lebanon, 350 plant species eke out an existence. Couchville Cedar Glade, adjacent to Long Hunter State Park, has the largest community of the endangered Tennessee coneflower.

In addition to the coneflower, flowering plant species living in these glades include the prickly pear cactus, limestone flame flower, Gattinger's prairie clover, glade phlox, and Nashville breadroot. Nonflowering plants include reindeer moss and glade moss. The clumps of reindeer moss are particularly noticeable because they live in small colonies. Along with the red cedar, trees in the surrounding forest include shagbark hickory and oak. Various rodents, birds, snakes, and an occasional wandering deer may be seen.

As early as 1901 botanists began noting the ecological importance of the cedar glades. Augustin Gattinger (1825–1903) mentioned the glades in his book *The Flora of Tennessee and the Philosophy of Botany*. Cedars of Lebanon State Park and the surrounding Cedars of Lebanon State Forest were designated a national natural landmark in 1973. This designation was based on research done by Elsie Quarterman of Vanderbilt University.

Cedars of Lebanon State Park: Cedar Woods Trail

This is a great hike for those interested in karst topography, with the numerous lime-stone outcrops and sinkholes adding a sense of adventure. In the spring the areas along the trail are ablaze with wildflowers. Several varieties of moss grow along the trail and even on the limestone. Limestone "steps" lead past a small seasonal pond. Watch for a 4-foot-high limestone wall.

Start: Cedar Woods Trail trailhead across the park road from Picnic Area 1

Distance: 2.1-mile lollipop

Approximate hiking time: 1 hour

Difficulty: Moderate due to some steep up-and-down areas

Trail surface: Dirt, rock

Best season: Year-round

Other trail users: Dog walkers

Canine compatibility: Leashed dogs permitted

Fees and permits: None required

Schedule: 8:00 a.m. to 10:00 p.m.

Maps: USGS: Vine; trail maps available at park headquarters and online at www.tnstateparks.com

Trail contact: Park Manager, Cedars of Lebanon State Park, 328 Cedar Forest Rd., Lebanon, TN 37090; (615) 443-2769; www.tnstateparks.com

Other: Water and restrooms are available at park headquarters and the picnic area. There is no potable water or restrooms on the trail. Take adequate water, use insect repellant, and wear a hat.

Finding the trailhead: From the south side of Nashville, take I-40 East toward Knoxville for 20 miles. Take US 231 South, exit 238, toward Lebanon/Hartsville and go 0.1 mile. Turn right onto US 231/South Cumberland Street/TN 10 and continue to follow US 231/TN 10 for 6.4 miles. Turn left on Cedar Forest Road; proceed 0.75 mile before turning left onto the Park Road, where you'll reach park headquarters in about 0.15 mile. *DeLorme Tennessee Atlas & Gazetteer:* Page 54, D2. GPS: N36 05.31' / W86 19.30'

The Cedar Woods Trail is located in the 900-acre Cedars of Lebanon State Park, in the heart of the middle Tennessee karst area. Hikers interested in learning more about karst topography will appreciate this hike. The trail is identified by white blazes on trees and directional signs at some of the Ys and Ts. This is the hilliest section of the park, with an elevation change of 100 feet. The hike is a "balloon on a string": The "string" section heads west as it leads to the Y at the "balloon" section, which is followed clockwise.

Stop at the park headquarters to get a trail map, then drive about 0.8 mile to the trailhead, which is across from Picnic Area 1 and near the junction of Cedar Forest Road and WPA Road. Start at the Cedar Woods Trail trailhead west of the picnic area, and head up an old asphalt road that forms the first 100 feet of the trail. Hardwoods and cedars are on both sides, and glimpses of the park road can be seen through the trees on the left. Bear right, heading north until reaching a Y, and take the left branch, heading west. This is the start of the loop section of the hike, which circles the northwestern section of the park.

Pass a cluster of shagbark hickory trees on both the right and left. In the fall nuts from the trees can be seen on the ground. Limestone "steps," flat outcrops of limestone, lead you to where the karst area begins in earnest. A karst is an area with

The Cedar Woods Trail in Cedars of Lebanon State Park winds up and down hills and passes limestone formations resembling walls.

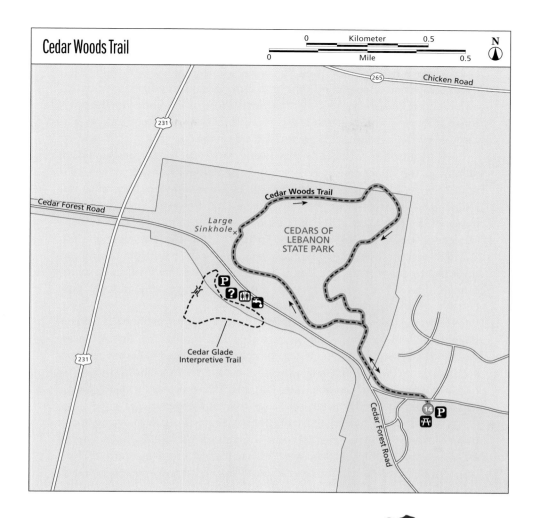

Cedar Woods Trail

0 — Kilometer — 0.5
0 — Mile — 0.5

N

Chicken Road
265

231

Cedar Forest Road

Cedar Woods Trail

Large
Sinkhole ×

CEDARS OF
LEBANON
STATE PARK

P
?

Cedar Glade
Interpretive Trail

231

Cedar Forest Road

14 P

Cedars of Lebanon State Park is named for the dense cedar forest that existed in the biblical lands of Lebanon. In 1995 the Cedar Lodge and several other structures built by the Civilian Conservation Corps in the 1930s and 1940s were placed on the National Register of Historic Places.

little or no topsoil, with limestone outcrops reaching to the surface. The under layer of limestone is gradually dissolved from water seeping through, allowing caves, passageways, and underground streams to form. This underground world has its own variety of flora and fauna. Over time the top layers of limestone over the caves collapse, forming sinkholes and crevasses, which are the signature features of a karst. Middle Tennessee has the largest karst area in the country.

The trail narrows to about 18 inches wide, with a dirt surface, and continues slightly up. The woods consist of cedars, oaks, and hickories. Bear right around a semicircle, still heading northwest, and pass by some large limestone outcrops, including rectangular blocks. Some of the limestone is grayish, almost like it was bleached. On the left side of the trail, a large block of flat-surfaced limestone about 18 inches high can be used as a bench. Follow the trail, which weaves right, left, and right again, by using the white blazes on the trees. The trail begins to level and slope slightly down. A few tree roots cross the trail, along with small rocks, so use caution. Moss can be seen in the woods and even clinging to limestone. This portion of the trail is the most strenuous part of the hike.

Follow the trail as it makes a hard right, heading north. Continue right, going slightly up. In the spring wildflowers are abundant in this area. Animal tracks, including deer, raccoon, and opossum, may be seen near the small seasonal pond you pass on the right. Zebra swallowtail, viceroy, and tiger swallowtail butterflies have also been spotted near the water. Portions of the trail may be muddy after a rain. Bear hard right and then left, still heading generally north.

A path on the right leads to a large sinkhole that is an excellent example of a major section of the limestone roof collapsing over a small cave. The sinkhole covers an area about 100 feet in diameter. Return to the trail after exploring the region around the sinkhole. Bear right, heading northeast, and almost immediately reach another large sinkhole, with a steep path going 8 feet down to the bottom of the hole. Use caution when using this path. The area offers many photo opportunities. Continue following the trail east, passing more sinkholes and outcrops, and then bear right, heading southwest until reaching a Y. Take the right branch and backtrack to the trailhead.

MILES AND DIRECTIONS

0.0 Start at the Cedar Woods Trail trailhead near Picnic Shelter 1 and across Cedar Forest Road. The trail is identified by white blazes painted on trees.

0.1 Head into the woods, going west. Cedar Forest Road can be seen on the left but is quickly hidden by the trees. After 400 feet reach a Y and take the left branch to follow the loop in a clockwise direction.

0.2 Reach a Y and take the right branch, heading northwest. There are trail markers and a white blaze at this Y. Follow the white-blazed trail slightly up as it weaves through the trees. Woods are on the right and left.

0.4 Pass some large outcrops of limestone and then go up several limestone "steps." Bear right, following the trail in a semicircle, going slightly up and heading generally west. Continue following the white blazes. Limestone outcrops are on both sides of the trail.

0.6 Follow the trail as it zigzags to the right and left, heading generally west and slightly up. Go up a few limestone "steps." This is the most strenuous section of the hike but not difficult. Continue following the white blazes.

0.7 Make a hard right, heading north and slightly up. Woods and limestone outcrops are on both sides of the trail. The trail begins to flatten as it passes a small seasonal pond on the right.

0.9 Bear slightly to the right, heading east and beginning to head down. Continue following the white blazes.

1.3 Make a hard right, then left, and reach a path to a large sinkhole on the right. Sections of the collapsed roof are in the hole. Explore around the sinkhole and return to the trail. Follow the white blazes and make a hard right, heading north.

1.5 Reach a path on the left that leads to another large sinkhole. A steep path about 8 feet long leads to the bottom. After investigating the sinkhole, return to the trail and continue following the white blazes south as the trail weaves through the woods. Pass a limestone outcrop that appears wall-like.

1.7 Pass several weirdly shaped outcrops and continue to follow the white blazes as the trail weaves through the woods.

2.0 Reach a Y and take the right branch, then backtrack to the trailhead.

2.1 End the hike at the trailhead.

The CCC's Impact on Parks

In 1933, with the country in the throes of the Great Depression, President Franklin D. Roosevelt established the Civilian Conservation Corps (CCC) to help combat unemployment. Little did he realize the lasting impact the CCC would have on our parks.

The young men working in the program constructed buildings, trails, and other infrastructure in city, state, and national parks that are still used today. Men from their upper teens through their early twenties worked in camps of about 200 men each for six-month periods and performed outdoor construction work. Few had any work experience beyond odd jobs, and most had completed one year or less of high school. Enrollees worked forty hours a week, were paid $30 a month, and were required to send $25 to their family. Groceries, fuel, equipment, and medical services were contracted locally. "This is a training station we're going to leave morally and physically fit to lick 'Old Man Depression,'" boasted the newsletter of one of the camps. The CCC became one of the most popular of Roosevelt's New Deal programs and was active in every state.

CCC labor allowed Tennessee to develop parklands at a scale not previously attainable. A number of state parks, utilizing the CCC, including Montgomery Bell and Cedars of Lebanon, are still operating. "We Get the Job Done" was the motto of Civilian Conservation Corps Camp 873. Several companies were assigned to work in Montgomery Bell State Park, Cedars of Lebanon State Park. and the Warner Parks. The cedar lodge in Cedars of Lebanon State Park was placed on the National Register of Historic Places, in 1995. Construction was done with locally available material including limestone and timber.

The CCC workforce peaked in August 1935, with 502,000 enrollees in 2,600 camps. By the time the corps was disbanded in 1942 due to World War II, more than three million men had participated. Their work had a lasting impact, still seen and utilized some seventy years later.

Cedars of Lebanon State Park: Cedar Glade Interpretive Trail

15

This is an excellent hike for families with young children or folks who are curious about cedar glades. Illustrated information signs along the edge of the trail explain the various features and creatures of a cedar glade. Several short bridges cross over wet areas containing a variety of birds and small mammals.

Start: Cedar Glade Interpretive Trail trailhead adjacent to the headquarters parking area

Distance: 0.6-mile counterclockwise loop

Approximate hiking time: 1 hour to allow time to read trail information signs

Difficulty: Easy due to flat trail and shade

Trail surface: Bark mulch, dirt, some asphalt

Best season: Year-round

Other trail users: Dog walkers

Canine compatibility: Leashed dogs permitted

Fees and permits: None required

Schedule: 8:00 a.m. to 10:00 p.m.

Maps: USGS: Vine; trail maps and interpretive brochures available at park headquarters

Trail contact: Park Manager, Cedars of Lebanon State Park, 328 Cedar Forest Rd., Lebanon, TN 37090; (615) 443-2769; www.state .tn.us/environment/parks

Other: Water and restrooms are available at park headquarters and the picnic area. There is no potable water or restrooms on the trail. Take adequate water, use insect repellant, and wear a hat.

Finding the trailhead: From the south side of Nashville, take I-40 East via the ramp on the left toward Knoxville for 20 miles. Take US 231 South, exit 238, toward Lebanon/Hartsville and go 0.1 mile. Turn right onto US 231/ South Cumberland Street/TN 10 and continue to follow US 231/TN 10 for 6.4 miles. Turn left on Cedar Forest Road, go 0.3 mile to 328 Cedar Forest Rd., Lebanon, and proceed to park headquarters. *DeLorme Tennessee Atlas & Gazetteer:* Page 54, D2. GPS: N36 05.51' / W86 19.88'

THE HIKE

The Cedar Glade Interpretive Trail is located in the 900-acre Cedars of Lebanon State Park, in the heart of the middle Tennessee karst area, which includes the cedar glades. Less than 100 square miles of functional cedar glade remain in the country. Hikers interested in learning more about cedar glades will appreciate this hike. The trail has a number of information signs describing the features of a cedar glade. Add another dimension to the hike by taking along a notepad to record information from the signs, noting glade features to watch for. The plant life in cedar glades has adapted to the harsh environment, with its thin to nonexistent topsoil underlaid with limestone. The glades in the state park and surrounding forest support several hundred different plant species.

From the trailhead adjacent to the parking area at the park headquarters, head west and almost immediately reach a covered kiosk. Turn right at the kiosk, temporarily heading north, then bear left until heading south. This short counterclockwise loop generally heads west, then south, then east, and finally northwest. Head slightly downhill into the woods, which have some hardwoods but are predominantly cedar. Bear left, then hard right, and pass an interpretive sign explaining the nature of cedar glades. Look for small clumps of reindeer moss, growing in circular clumps 12 to 15 inches in diameter and 8 to 12 inches high. Bear hard left at the interpretive sign and head slightly down.

Pass the second interpretive sign, which describes some geological features of the cedar glade. Almost immediately cross a short bridge over a seasonal creek and

The Cedar Glade Interpretive Trail furnishes examples of karst topography, including crevasses and sinkholes.

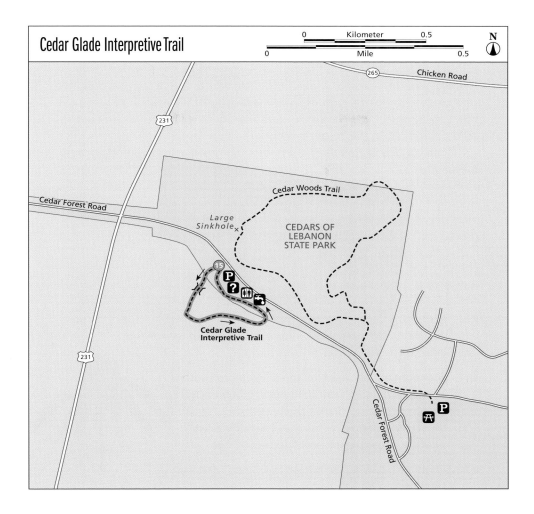

Cedar Glade Interpretive Trail

0   Kilometer   0.5

0   Mile   0.5

N

265 Chicken Road

231

Cedar Woods Trail

Cedar Forest Road

Large
Sinkhole ×

CEDARS OF
LEBANON
STATE PARK

15
P
?

Cedar Glade
Interpretive Trail

231

Cedar Forest Road

P

bear slightly to the right. With all this weaving right and left, the trail leads generally south. Pass another interpretive sign that lists some plants common to glades. Woods, now predominantly oak and hickory, still border the trail but furnish no shade. In the spring look for the limestone flame flower and Gattinger's prairie clover. The clover has a yellow center and white petals.

The trail zigzags as it continues to head generally east. In the spring look for butterflies, including yellow and white sulphurs, viceroys, and tiger swallowtails. They like to congregate around small puddles of water. Pass another interpretive sign. Look into the woods and try to identify some of the trees, which include the winged elm, with its gray bark with shallow fissures and its small, toothed leaves. The redbud is also in these woods, recognized by its heart-shaped leaves and in the fall by its bean-pod-like fruit that is 2 to 3 inches long. Also present are Carolina buckthorn, black haw, and bushy sumac.

Pass a sinkhole that is 5 feet from the left side of the trail. The hole is about 90 feet long and 25 feet wide. Use caution when going past these holes. Continue heading generally east and then nearly double back as the trail follows obliquely northwest. Listen for the raucous cry of the blue jay. This medium-size bird often tries to bully other birds. The call *pic-a-tuk* identifies the summer tanager, and its solid rosy red color makes it easy to spot.

Continue heading northwest and watch for small animals, including frogs, salamanders, lizards, and rabbits. Pass another interpretive sign and follow the trail as it heads up a slight slope. Bear left and right as the trail weaves between the trees. Take the time to inspect the rotting tree stumps that adjoin the trail, looking for insects, lichen, and fungus. Pass an information sign that honors Dr. Elsie Quarterman and her work in preserving the cedar glades before reaching the trailhead and ending the hike.

MILES AND DIRECTIONS

0.0 Start at the Cedar Glade Interpretive Trail trailhead at the edge of the parking area by the park headquarters and head west to walk the loop counterclockwise.

0.1 Turn right at the kiosk near the trailhead and within 100 yards bear left and then hard right, passing an interpretive sign listing six characteristics of a cedar glade. Bear left at the sign. The trail weaves a little as it leads to the next interpretive sign.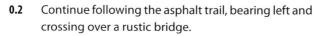

0.2 Continue following the asphalt trail, bearing left and crossing over a rustic bridge.

0.3 Reach a long, straight, easy grade, heading down. Pass an interpretive sign on the left and bear right, heading east from the sign. Pass a large sinkhole about 5 feet off the trail, bearing left around the edge. Pass a clearing on the left.

0.4 Follow the trail generally heading east. Make a hard left and reach an interpretive sign. A large clearing is behind the sign. The trail weaves a bit and passes two more interpretive signs.

0.5 The trail leads straight ahead and up a minor slope. Pass another interpretive sign and bear left, then immediately right. Continue following the trail as it heads generally northwest. Bear left, going slightly down and then right until reaching an interpretive sign. Follow the trail going north, toward the trailhead.

0.6 End the hike at the trailhead.

Cedars of Lebanon State Park: Limestone Sink Trail

This self-guided trail through a limestone sink area is an interesting and educational look at karst topography. It is a good hike for families with young children. Sinkholes and small crevasses provide great photo ops. Some of the sinkholes are large enough to climb down into and explore. Several varieties of ferns and wildflowers can be seen, and be sure to check out the large warts (burls) on the tree at station 10.

Start: Limestone Sink Trailhead adjacent to the parking area just past the swimming pool

Distance: 0.6-mile clockwise loop

Approximate hiking time: 1 hour to allow time to read interpretive signs

Difficulty: Easy due to flat shaded trail

Trail surface: Stone, rock, gravel

Best season: Year-round

Other trail users: Dog walkers

Canine compatibility: Leashed dogs permitted

Fees and permits: None required

Schedule: 8:00 a.m. to 10:00 p.m.

Maps: USGS: Vine; trail maps and brochures available at park headquarters

Trail contact: Park Manager, Cedars of Lebanon State Park, 328 Cedar Forest Rd., Lebanon, TN 37090; (615) 443-2769; www.state .tn.us/environment/parks

Other: Water and restrooms are available at park headquarters and the picnic area. There is no potable water or restrooms on the trail. Take adequate water, use insect repellant and sunscreen, and wear a hat. No bicycles allowed.

Finding the trailhead: From the south side of Nashville, take I-40 East via the ramp on the left toward Knoxville for 20 miles. Take US 231 South, exit 238, toward Lebanon/ Hartsville and go 0.1 mile. Turn right onto US 231/South Cumberland Street/TN 10 and continue to follow US 231/TN 10 for 6.4 miles. Turn left on Cedar Forest Road, go 0.3 mile to 328 Cedar Forest Rd., Lebanon, and proceed to park headquarters. *DeLorme Tennessee Atlas & Gazetteer:* Page 54, D2. GPS: N36 04.71' / W86 18.8'

THE HIKE

The Limestone Sink Trail is located in the 900-acre Cedars of Lebanon State Park, in the heart of the middle Tennessee karst area. Sinkholes are one of the signature features of karst topography. Hikers interested in learning more about karst features will appreciate this short hike. Add another dimension to the hike by taking along a notepad to record information from the interpretive signs.

Stop at the park office to pick up a map and interpretive guide before starting your hike at the Limestone Sink Trail trailhead, which is adjacent to the parking area just past the swimming pool. Take the left branch at the Y at the trailhead; this will keep the interpretive signs in the order they are listed in the guide. The trail is identified by blue blazes on trees. Cedars and hardwood trees, including oak and hickory, furnish good cover from the sun. Use caution along the trail, as the entire area is covered with sinkholes, crevasses, limestone outcrops, and limestone blocks. Learn to recognize poison ivy, for this noxious plant borders much of the trail.

Reach a path on the left that leads to a large sinkhole with big hardwood trees growing from the bottom and sides of it. The hole is 30 feet wide and 90 feet long, with sharply sloping sides. The more adventurous can sidestep to the bottom to investigate the structure. Return to the main trail and almost immediately reach a path on the right side that leads to large limestone outcrops and a small sinkhole.

This is an example of a sinkhole created by the collapse of the 4-foot thick limestone roof over a cave.

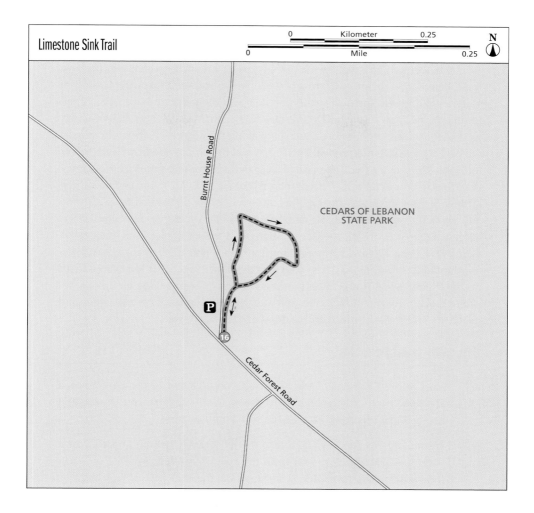

CEDARS OF LEBANON
STATE PARK

Burnt House Road

Cedar Forest Road

P

16

The area around the outcrops can also be explored. Return to the main trail and in a short distance reach Interpretive Sign 2; bear hard left at the sign. Amazingly, this has all happened in 0.1 mile!

Follow the trail, with its blue blazes, as it weaves between the trees and limestone. In a short distance bear right, heading generally northeast. Pass Interpretive Sign 3 on the right and bear slightly left. In the spring small butterflies congregate in this area. They are most noticeable after a rain near small puddles of water. Ferns, including the Christmas fern, can be seen in the woods. Pass the remains of a small sinkhole on the left, about 10 feet from the trail. Broken pieces of limestone have filled most of the hole, and large blocks of limestone surround it, like guarding sentinels. A path leads to the area, allowing investigation.

The trail zigzags around trees and limestone slabs and outcrops. Interpretive Sign 4 was not seen—it may have been destroyed and not replaced. Pass Interpretive

16

Sign 5 and reach a large sinkhole, about 90 feet in diameter, with a limestone wall about 25 feet behind it. Follow the trail as it bears left and proceeds into the sinkhole. Bear hard right at the bottom of the sinkhole and keep following the trail as it leads up and out. The next section of the trail is the most strenuous. Pass Interpretive Sign 6 on the right and a large sinkhole about 150 feet long, 40 feet across, and 15 feet deep. Use caution in following along the edge of the hole and almost immediately reach Interpretive Sign 7. A wood bench provided by Eagle Scouts of Troop 387 provides a good place to sit a spell and contemplate nature's work.

Reach a Y and take the right branch, generally heading south, and pass Interpretive Signs 8 and 9. Stay clear of the poison ivy bordering the trail. Stop to examine the huge, nearly 5 feet in diameter, hardwood tree at Interpretive Sign 10. The large wartlike growths on the tree are burls. In a short distance pass Interpretive Signs 11, 12, and 13. Go down some limestone steps and follow the trail past Interpretive Signs 14 and 15. Reach a Y and take the right branch (the left branch leads to the Hidden Springs Trail). Pass Interpretive Sign 16 near a large group of limestone blocks, 2 to 4 feet high. Bear left after going up some limestone steps and reach a Y. Take the left branch and backtrack to the trailhead.

MILES AND DIRECTIONS

0.0 Start at the Limestone Sinks Trail trailhead adjacent to the parking area and head north. The trail is a narrow loop, traveling mostly north and then south, and is identified by blue blazes painted on trees.

0.1 Within 200 feet reach a Y and take the left branch, heading north. Pass a large sinkhole about 15 feet from the trail on the left. A short path leads to its edge. Continue on the trail and pass Interpretive Signs 1, and 2. Bear hard left at sign 2 and immediately bear hard right and pass Interpretive Sign 3.

0.2 Pass a sinkhole about 10 feet to the left with 2-foot-high limestone blocks surrounding it. A short path leads to it, allowing investigation. Continue north and almost immediately pass another large sinkhole and crevasse. Pass Interpretive Signs 4 and 5 while following the blue-blazed trail, then bear south.

0.3 Pass Interpretive Sign 6 on the right and a large sinkhole about 150 feet long by 40 feet wide and 15 feet deep. Use caution. At Interpretive Sign 7 and the bench, continue heading south, following the blue blazes. This is the most difficult section of the trail.

0.4 Reach a Y and take the right branch, then pass Interpretive Signs 8 and 9. Reach Interpretive Sign 10 and a tall hardwood tree with huge burls. Bear hard left at the tree, still heading generally south and passing Interpretive Signs 11, 12, and 13.

0.5 Pass Interpretive Signs 14 and 15 on the right, still following the blue-blazed trail. Immediately reach a Y and take the right branch toward the trailhead. Bear slightly to the left and backtrack on the very short connector to the trailhead.

0.6 End the hike at the trailhead.

What's a Burl?

I had gone over to my son Scott's house to see if he and Austin, his twelve-year-old son, were interested in a hike. I asked if they wanted to look at some pretty neat burls on an Osage orange tree at Carnton Plantation and a large oak in Cedars of Lebanon State Park. Scott is a carpenter and had studied numerous woods.

"What's a burl?" Austin asked, to which I replied, "It's kinda like a wart on a tree, but your dad's worked with burls, so he probably knows." Scott was quick to answer, "It's where the grain has grown in a deformed way. It usually happens when the tree has undergone some type of stress from insects or some molds. Burls can be both above and below the ground. Sometimes the burls aren't discovered until the tree dies or falls over. This wood is pretty expensive, used in upscale pipes, bowls, and ornamental pens and as inlays on furniture. It's also quite rare, adding to its cost. Burl wood is very hard to work in a lathe, because its grain is misshapen and not straight. Mom got me started in working with burl, when she gave me a pen made from Ohio buckeye."

Austin asked, "Can fruit trees have burls, say like an apple tree?" Scott answered, "I think so, but let's look on the Internet." Austin suggested that since we were going to see an oak and an Osage orange, we should also look for those on the Internet. He fired up his computer and got us online. He first looked up apple burl, and sure enough, apple trees can have burls. Then he queried Osage orange, and we all began reading.

One of the first bits of history we learned was that Osage orange trees were one of the primary trees used in President Franklin D. Roosevelt's "Great Plains Shelterbelt," or windbreaks. This was a Works Progress Administration (WPA) jobs program started in 1934, in the midst of the Great Depression. When the windbreak program ended in 1942, 220 million trees had been planted. The article noted that the sharp-thorned trees were also planted to keep cattle in their pastures. Scott commented, "Hey, I remember when we lived in Illinois and there were rows of Osage orange trees separating farmers' fields. We called their fruit 'hedge apples.' I didn't know about burls then, or I could have had a great collection."

Next we read that in Arkansas in the early nineteenth century, a good Osage bow was worth a horse and a blanket. Burls, however, were a detriment and not appreciated. Austin was getting eager to see some burls and called out, "Grandpa, can we stop the history and get going? I'll bring my camera." I smiled, pleased with his interest, and told Austin and Scott that we would go to Carnton Plantation first (hike18).

Upon arriving at Carnton, we immediately went to the garden area where the Osage orange was located. When Austin saw the tree, he was impressed. "Wow! Those look like big warts. They must be 3 feet across and sticking out 2 feet." I told Scott and Austin that Justin, the head gardener at Carnton, had told me that the tree was about 160 years old. Scott said that meant it was here during the Civil War's Battle of Franklin, in 1864. Then he said, "I've worked with several types of burl, and Osage orange is one of the easiest to work with. Besides, it smells nice and takes a beautiful finish." Austin was busy taking pictures and feeling the burl.

I called out, "OK, gang, let's get going to Cedars of Lebanon, because seeing the burl there requires a short hike." Arriving at the park, we picked up an interpretive brochure and headed toward Interpretative Sign 10 on the Limestone Sink Trail. The large oak tree came into view in a small clearing. Both Scott and Austin were stopped in their tracks when they saw the tree. Scott spoke first, "Dad, there are two huge burls on the tree and there may be more underground! I can't even imagine how much useable burl there is." Austin just stood there, wide-eyed and snapping pictures, and finally commented, "This is something else. Can we hurry home so I can download my pictures?" Scott and I smiled and nodded our heads in agreement.

Vesta Cedar Glade State Natural Area

This hike will especially appeal to those who want to learn a lot about cedar glades in a short time. Vesta contains cedar glades, barrens, cedar-hardwood forest, and the endangered Tennessee coneflower—all within a relatively small area. The flat landscape features exposed limestone outcrops and sinkholes that add interest. Be prepared to hike on a primitive grass trail.

Start: Vesta Cedar Glade Trail trailhead adjacent to the small gravel parking area
Distance: 1.5-mile counterclockwise loop
Approximate hiking time: 1 hour
Difficulty: Easy due to flat surface
Trail surface: Dirt, grass
Best season: September to June
Other trail users: Dog walkers
Canine compatibility: Leashed dogs permitted

Fees and permits: None required
Schedule: Dawn to dusk
Maps: USGS: Gladeville
Trail contact: Division of Natural Areas, 401 Church St., 7th floor L&C Annex, Nashville, TN 37243; (615) 532-0431; www.tnstateparks .com
Other: There is no potable water or restrooms on the trail. Take adequate water and use sunscreen and insect repellant.

Finding the trailhead: From the south side of Nashville, take I-40 eastbound about 28 miles to exit at TN 231. Proceed south for approximately 9 miles and turn right on Vesta Road, then go approximately 2 miles and turn right onto Moccasin Road. Continue approximately 1 mile to the small parking area on the left. *DeLorme Tennessee Atlas & Gazetteer:* Page 54, D2. GPS: N36 04.60' / W86 23.75'

THE HIKE

The Vesta Cedar Glade Trail is in the 150-acre Vesta Cedar Glade State Natural Area, located in the southwest corner of Cedars of Lebanon State Park. The Tennessee Division of Forestry and Division of Natural Areas cooperatively manage the area. Cedar glades, barrens, cedar-hardwood forest, limestone outcrops, and sinkholes surround the trail. This is karst topography, and it strongly influences the cedar glade ecology. These glades present an excellent example of middle Tennessee's most unique natural areas. Vesta is especially noteworthy due to the abundance of federally endangered Tennessee coneflower that it supports.

Although the glades look rugged, they are very fragile. When hiking, tread lightly and avoid trampling the flowers and grasses. Some species of plants that grow in these glades can be found nowhere else in the world, and many are on the endangered species list. Because of their uniqueness, the cedar glades are known and valued by naturalists around the world.

Start at the Vesta Cedar Glade Trail trailhead adjacent to the four-car parking area off of Moccasin Road. Go through the gate and head north on this 1.5-mile counterclockwise loop. The first mile of the primitive mowed-grass trail is well signed with marker posts and blue blazes, and the folks at the Division of Natural Areas are working to sign the last half mile. The trail follows along a fence that encloses a restricted-access ten-acre plot that protects the endangered Tennessee coneflower. The trail then leads into the woods, which can have a large population of mosquitoes after a rain.

In about 300 feet reach a kiosk that contains a large map of the glade. Study the map to become familiar with the trail. Follow the mowed trail until reaching a T; take the right branch, heading north on a short out and back to a clearing. Trees and undergrowth line the edge of the trail. The clearing is about 300 by 400 feet,

Insects obtain nectar from daisies growing in the normally barren cedar glade.

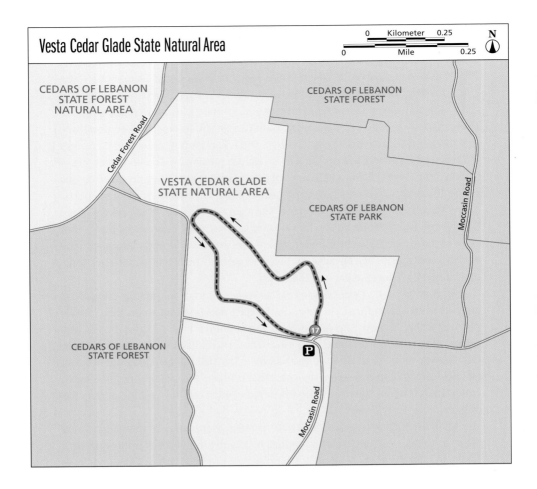

and in the spring wildflowers, including daisies, cover this area. Take time to investigate the clearing, which is unusual in a cedar glade, then backtrack to the T and take the right branch, which leads into the woods. The woods are predominantly oak mixed with a few cedars. In the spring watch for dragonflies pursuing mosquitoes. The trail veers right, then left, and back right.

Break into a small opening that has small rocks and gravel on the limestone surface. This is typical karst terrain. A karst has little or no soil on the surface and is underlaid with limestone. Rain and groundwater seeping through the surface eventually erodes the limestone, creating caves, sinkholes, and underground streams. Karsts have their own distinct species of flora and fauna. Follow the trail as it bears left, heading northwest. The tree canopy furnishing shade is intermittent. Wildflowers, including pale blue glade phlox, carpet some of the rocky limestone outcrops.

Cross a narrow seasonal stream and turn hard right. The woods are now mostly cedar and about 25 feet away. Pass a directional marker post, and look for animal tracks near any water. The area is not good habitat for mammals, but a few deer live in the woods. Continue following the blue blazes and trail marker posts until reaching a clearing that's about 250 feet in diameter. Wildflowers, including masses of Gattinger's petalostemon, with its rose-purple flowers, bloom in early June.

Walk across the clearing to pick up the trail on the opposite side. If the grass is tall, use a walking stick (could be any branch) and brush the grass. Snakes, including the venomous rattlesnake, call this territory home, but they are not aggressive and during the heat of the day will be seeking shade elsewhere. No snakebites have been reported here. Look for clusters of Tennessee milk vetch, with its pale yellow flowers. The trail leads into the cedars, heading toward the fence enclosing the ten acres of Tennessee coneflowers. Follow the trail along the fence to the trailhead.

MILES AND DIRECTIONS

0.0 Start at the Vesta Cedar Glade Trail trailhead adjacent to the four-car parking area and head north.

0.1 Follow the grass trail, with the park boundary fence on the right. About 1 mile of the trail has blue blazes painted on trees. Reach a T and take the right branch, heading northeast. The path becomes indistinct and overgrown. Bear slightly right and break out into a large clearing.

0.2 Backtrack to the T and trail marker post and take the right branch, heading into the woods.

0.3 Bear right, then left, and immediately right, heading generally north.

0.5 Continue following the narrow grass trail as it bears left at a trail marker post. The trail heads generally left and reaches a trail marker on the right. Bear left at the marker, heading northwest and watching for the blue blazes.

0.6 Cross a shallow seasonal stream and turn hard right, heading north. Continue following the trail until reaching a trail marker and temporarily bear right, to the northeast.

0.8 Reach a circular clearing about 250 feet in diameter. Continue across the clearing and pick up the trail on the opposite side, heading southeast.

1.3 Follow the trail as it weaves through cedar trees. It then proceeds straight ahead until making a hard right, east, quickly followed by left, right, and left. The trail then approaches the boundary fence, at which point it joins the original trail. Backtrack toward the trailhead.

1.5 End the hike at the trailhead.

East Flank—Battle of Franklin

This is a great hike for Civil War buffs. Walk the fields where the historic Battle of Franklin was fought on November 30, 1864, and follow Saw Mill Creek, which harbors a beaver lodge. The trail leads past Carnton Plantation, which was used as a Confederate field hospital and later gained fame in the novel Widow of the South.

Start: Unmarked trailhead adjacent to paved parking area
Distance: 2-mile clockwise loop
Approximate hiking time: 1 hour
Difficulty: Easy due to flat paved trails
Trail surface: Asphalt, grass
Best season: September to June
Other trail users: Dog walkers, bird-watchers
Canine compatibility: Leashed dogs permitted
Fees and permits: None required

Schedule: Dawn to dusk
Maps: USGS: Franklin
Trail contact: Manager, Carnton Plantation, 1345 Carnton Lane, Franklin, TN 37064; (615) 794-0903; www.Carnton.org
Other: Restrooms and water are available at the Carnton Plantation. There is no potable water or restrooms on the trail. Much of the hike is without shade. Take adequate water, use sunscreen and insect repellant, and wear a hat.

Finding the trailhead: From the south side of Nashville, take I-40 East via the ramp on the left toward Knoxville and go 0.9 mile. Merge onto I-65 South via exit 210 toward Huntsville and go 16.9 miles. Take TN 96, exit 65, toward Franklin and go 0.2 miles. Turn right onto Murfreesboro Road and go 1.1 mile, then turn left onto Mack Hatcher Memorial Parkway and go 1.4 miles. Turn right onto Lewisburg Pike and go 1.4 miles, then take a sharp left turn onto Carnton Lane and go 0.5 mile to 1345 Carnton Lane in Franklin. Turn left into the parking area for the trailhead. *DeLorme Tennessee Atlas & Gazetteer:* Pag 37, A5. GPS: N35 54.35' / W86 51.75'

18

Hikers interested in learning more about a major Civil War battle will appreciate this hike. The Harpeth River borders the north side of trail but cannot be seen. Much of the trail is in the hiker's line of sight. The trail is wheelchair and stroller accessible and is being revised and upgraded with informational signs covering the battle.

This trail was created in 2010 using part of a golf course that covered much of the eastern flank of the Battle of Franklin. The battle, one of the bloodiest of the

Fording a creek adds interest to the hike around the east flank of the Civil War Battle of Franklin.

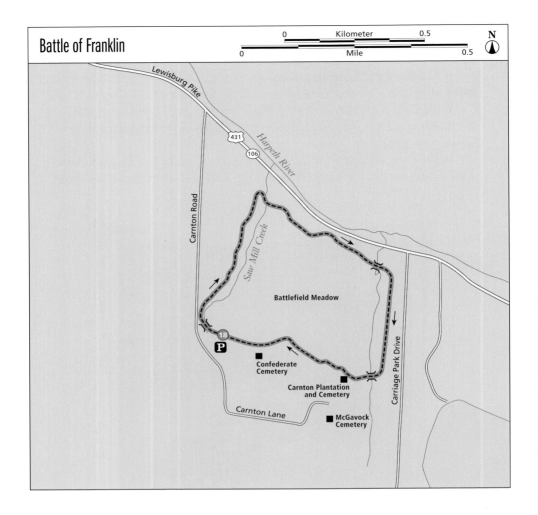

Civil War, was waged on November 30, 1864. Confederate General John Bell Hood ordered thirteen charges across open fields and a well-fortified Franklin. A quarter of his army was decimated, with 6,250 Confederate soldiers killed, wounded, or missing. Six Confederate generals died and were laid out to await burial on the porch of Carnton Plantation, which was used as a Confederate field hospital during the battle. This battle, along with Union General William Tecumseh Sherman's March to the Sea, signaled the beginning of the end of the Confederates' organized fighting. Reading about the Battle of Franklin prior to hiking this trail will add an extra dimension to the hike.

Begin your hike at the unmarked trailhead adjacent to the paved parking area and head northwest. Residences can be seen across Carnton Road on the right. Bear right and almost immediately cross a bridge on the right over McGavock

Creek. The creek is clear and shallow, about 10 to 18 inches deep, and leads to the central section of the battlefield. The trail heads slightly up, with small groups of hardwood trees on the right and left and mowed grass around the entire area of the trail. The *coo coo coo* of mourning doves can be heard throughout the year. The doves congregate on the ground and are easy to observe because they have become accustomed to people. Follow the trail up and over a low hill to a T. Take the left branch, heading north. Bear left past a line of trees, with the creek about 20 feet away on the right. Black willow and cottonwood trees are among the hardwoods bordering its bank.

Continue following the trail, which switches from concrete to asphalt. Small groups of hardwood trees are scattered around the area. The grounds were virtually devoid of trees at the time of the Battle of Franklin. There was little hand-to-hand combat during the battle, just the devastating cannon fire from the Union lines raining down on the charging Confederate troops. It was reported that the ground was covered with bodies and the creek turned red from the blood. The scene is hard to visualize in today's sublime surroundings.

Turn right, heading east and down a slight slope to the creek. A white fence on the left marks the park's boundary. After reaching the creek, turn right and follow the trail as it runs parallel to the stream, which is bordered by a few limestone slabs. In a short distance look for a series of flat stones crossing the creek. These are used to ford it, adding a bit of interest to the hike. Pleasant gurgling sounds come from the flowing water as it rushes around the rocks. Reach a T with a concrete walk-around and follow it left toward the boundary fence. Continue along the trail as it zigzags right, left, and back right, generally heading east along the park boundary on the left. Hardwood trees, including oak and maple, and bushes shield the boundary. Enjoy the shade furnished by the trees.

Go down a slight hill and immediately cross a bridge over the creek. Continue along the trail and make a hard right, heading south. Reach a path on the right and follow it to a bridge. While crossing the bridge, notice the pond on the right, which was created by beavers' building a dam across the creek. In a short distance the trail makes a hard right, heading west. Carnton Plantation and the Confederate cemetery are adjacent to the left side of the trail. Take time to visit Carnton Plantation and its garden. A three-trunked osage orange tree that was planted before the civil war, is in the garden. Look for the large burls located on the trunk. Continue to the trailhead.

> *A beaver can cut down a 3-inch tree in ten minutes. The trees are then used to build a dam and the beaver's lodge.*

0.0   Start at the unmarked trailhead at the northwest corner of the parking area and head northwest to make a clockwise loop.

0.1   Follow the concrete trail as it bears slightly right, heading generally northwest, and crosses a bridge over Saw Mill Creek. The creek is on the right and Carnton Road is on the left.

0.2   Bear right, heading northeast. After a short distance bear left, heading northwest, and almost immediately bear right, heading north and crossing a bridge .

0.4   Continue following the trail north until it doubles back on itself, then proceed a short distance and ford a shallow creek. After fording the creek, make a hard left, heading north, and almost immediately make a hard right, heading east. The Harpeth River is to the left but cannot be seen.

0.8   Continue following the trail, generally east. Trees are on the left, and the battlefield meadow is on the right. Reach a T and take the left branch, heading south. Pass a stone bench and continue following the trail south as it meanders. The left side parallels a road.

1.0   Reach a Y and take the left branch, still following generally south.

1.5   Follow the trail generally south, crossing a bridge with a beaver dam and impoundment on the right. Continue following the trail until it takes a hard right, heading west.

1.7   Pass the Carnton Plantation buildings and cemetery, both on the left. Take time to visit the plantation. Continue following the trail west until reaching the parking area.

2.0   End the hike at the parking area.

> **🌱 Green Tip:**
> *Be courteous of others. Many people visit natural areas for quiet, peace, and solitude, so avoid making loud noises and intruding on others' privacy.*

Pinkerton Park: Fort Granger Trail

Civil War buffs will enjoy this hike that leads to a 40-foot-high bluff above the Harpeth River, overlooking Franklin. Stairs and a boardwalk assist in the hike up the steep, heavily wooded hillside to the location of the fort, which was constructed in 1863 by Union soldiers. Signs along the trail provide interesting information about the fort, which no longer exists.

Start: Fort Granger Trail trailhead adjacent to the parking area
Distance: 1.1 miles out and back, with a small clockwise loop
Approximate hiking time: 1 hour to allow time to read information signs
Difficulty: Moderate due to some steep slopes and stairs
Trail surface: Dirt, grass
Best season: Year-round
Other trail users: Joggers, dog walkers
Canine compatibility: Leashed dogs permitted

Fees and permits: None required
Schedule: Dawn to dusk
Maps: USGS: Franklin
Trail contact: Franklin Parks and Recreation, 705 Boyd Mill Avenue, Franklin, TN 37064; (615) 790-5885; www.wcparksandrec.com
Other: Water and restrooms are available in Pinkerton Park. There is no potable water or restrooms on the trail. Much of the trail is without shade, so take adequate water, use sunscreen and insect repellant, and wear a hat.

Finding the trailhead: From the south side of Nashville, take I-40 East via the ramp on the left toward Knoxville and go 0.9 mile. Merge onto I-65 South via exit 210 toward Huntsville and go 16.9 miles. Take TN 96, exit 65, toward Franklin and go 0.2 mile. Turn right onto Murfreesboro Road and go 2.2 miles to 405 Murfreesboro Rd., Franklin, on the right. Proceed to the parking area. *DeLorme Tennessee Atlas & Gazetteer:* Page 37, A5. GPS: N35 55.35' / W86 51.73'

Hikers interested in learning more about a Union fort built to protect Franklin during the Civil War will appreciate this hike. The fort is gone, but information signs tell where buildings were located, the placement of guns, and other interesting data. The fort was an earthwork structure, 781 feet long and 346 feet wide, covering nearly twelve acres. It took three months to construct the fort in 1863, from March to May. The sentry/observation trail on the edge of the bluff is intact, furnishing a view down the hill toward Franklin. Fort Granger is located on 40-foot-high Figuer's Bluff, above the Harpeth River overlooking Franklin. Figuer's Bluff joins the north side of Pinkerton Park.

This is the trail, overlooking Franklin, used by sentries from Union troops who were defending Fort Granger during the Civil War.

The nearly 8,000 soldiers stationed at the fort during the Battle of Franklin on November 30, 1864, had ringside seats to one of the bloodiest battles of the Civil War. A four-gun battery inside the fort, commanded by Giles Cockerill, pummeled Major General William W. Loring's Confederate troops with devastating fire as they attempted to advance across the eastern flank of the battlefield. At least 163 rounds from the battery rained down on the troops. One of the men stationed at the fort, Captain Alonzo D. Harvey, commanding the Fifteenth Indiana Battery, observed, "As Fort Granger was on a high hill, we had the most beautiful sight of the bloodiest battle that has been fought since gunpowder has been invented— the battle of Franklin."

The half-mile trail to the Fort Granger site is an out-and–back hike with a small balloon. The outbound section heads generally northeast and then north, while the inbound section heads generally south and then southwest. A meander of the Harpeth River, small hills, limestone outcrops and steps, a boardwalk, and the fort site with information signs are features of the hike. The Tinkerbell playground and a picnic area, which may be an incentive to hikers with young children, are adjacent to the parking area in Pinkerton Park.

The hike starts at the Fort Granger Trail trailhead, which is reached by following a sidewalk north from the parking area. A FORT GRANGER sign is located near the Y at the trailhead. Take the left branch, go down a slight slope, and immediately reach a bridge crossing a meander of the Harpeth River. The water is clear and 6 to12 inches deep, depending on the amount of rainfall. A canoe access on the left allows launching into the river. The area is mowed, and there are electric utility lines overhead. Reach a clearing 150 feet wide by 300 feet deep and continue following the narrow dirt trail across the clearing. Pass the Outdoor Learning Center and immediately reach a steep set of steps, with limestone outcrops along and below them. Continue up the steps, passing a bench, and reach the boardwalk. The boardwalk is long, with a set of steps. Bear right and reach a large observation area, 10 feet wide and 20 feet long. One view from the observation area is of trees, while the other shows power lines.

As you continue on the boardwalk, notice a small depression in the limestone to the right, about 7 feet by 7 feet. Exit the boardwalk by a set of steps leading to the former sentry path adjoining Fort Granger along the top of the bluff. During the battle the hill overlooking Franklin was bare, but it is now covered by trees and undergrowth. Follow this path northwest and try to imagine what it was like being

---

🌿 Green Tip:
When choosing trail snacks, go with homemade goodies that aren't packaged.

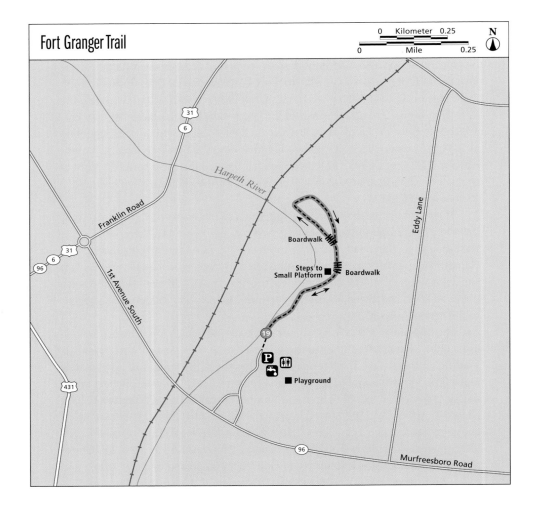

a soldier on sentry duty. Follow to the right and up a small incline to the grounds of the fort. There is no trail through the fort area, so just go from information sign to information sign, eventually heading back toward the boardwalk.

One of the most interesting signs discusses Fort Granger's history. It notes there was a 9,000-gallon cistern near the sign—that's a lot of water, since many rural homes today consider a 500-gallon cistern very large. Hardwood trees, including oak and maple, are scattered throughout the fort grounds, furnishing small amounts of shade. Continue investigating the information signs until reaching the boardwalk and backtracking to the trailhead.

0.0 Start at the Fort Granger Trail trailhead, just north of the Pinkerton Park parking area, and head north to the Y and take the left branch.

0.1 Almost immediately cross a bridge over a meander of the Harpeth River, which is on the left. Follow the trail, heading northeast. Reach and cross a clearing, walking under power lines.

0.2 Reach stairs leading up a steep hill and almost immediately reach a boardwalk that overlooks the area.

0.3 Go up another set of stairs, which include some limestone "steps." There is a bench at the end of the steps. Continue following the trail as it veers generally north.

0.5 Reach the top of the bluff and a Y and take the right branch. Fort Granger was situated to the right; the city of Franklin is down the slope to the left but cannot be seen. Continue following the narrow trail as it bears right and up a small hill to the Fort Granger site.

0.7 Reach the fort site, which does not contain a trail. Investigate the information signs, following in a north, then east, and finally south direction, leading back to the boardwalk and steps.

0.8 Reach the boardwalk at the southern boundary of the fort and backtrack to the trailhead. Use caution going down the stairs.

1.1 End the hike at the trailhead.

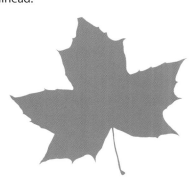

Franklin Greenway: Aspen Grove Trail

This is a great trail for creek lovers and bird-watchers, as well as families with young children. Bridges, woods, a small wetlands, and Spencer Creek add special interest. Only by passing some office buildings and a shopping mall are you reminded that this is an in-city hike.

Start: Unmarked Aspen Grove Trail trailhead at the east side of the parking area
Distance: 1.1-mile lollipop
Approximate hiking time: 1 hour
Difficulty: Easy due to flat paved trail
Trail surface: Asphalt
Best season: Year-round
Other trail users: Dog walkers, joggers, skateboarders, strollers, wheelchairs
Canine compatibility: Leashed dogs allowed

Fees and permits: None required
Schedule: Dawn to dusk
Maps: USGS: Franklin
Trail contact: Franklin Parks and Recreation Department, 705 Boyd Mill Ave., Franklin, TN 37064; (615) 794-2103; www.wcparksandrec .com
Other: Water and restrooms are available next to the parking area. There is no potable water or restrooms on the trail. Take adequate water, use insect repellant and sunscreen, and wear a hat.

Finding the trailhead: From the south side of Nashville, take I-40 East via the ramp on the left toward Knoxville and go 0.9 mile. Merge onto I-65 South via exit 210 toward Huntsville and go 14.4 miles. Take West Cool Springs Boulevard, exit 68B, and go 0.5 mile, then merge onto Cool Springs Boulevard and go 0.7 mile. Turn right onto Aspen Grove Drive and proceed 0.2 mile to 3200 Aspen Grove Dr., Franklin, and the parking area and trailhead. *DeLorme Tennessee Atlas & Gazetteer:* Page 37, A5. GPS: N35 56.81' / W86 49.84'

THE HIKE

The 1.1-mile counterclockwise loop forming the Aspen Grove Trail is located in the fourteen-acre Aspen Grove Park in the Cool Springs area of Franklin. Even though the park is rather small, the trail leads through woods and along Spencer Creek, giving the illusion of a much larger area. The accessible path is 12 feet wide and paved for multiple users. Stay on the right side of the trail to give other users the opportunity to pass. Always give notice when passing people (on the left) using strollers or wheelchairs. Benches and a few picnic tables are conveniently placed along the trail. The playground, pavilion, and picnic area near the parking area may be an incentive to hikers with young children.

Begin your hike at the unmarked Aspen Grove Trail trailhead at the east side of the parking area, and follow the sidewalk east until reaching a T. A shelter and playground are on the left; go to the right and head toward a bridge over Spencer Creek. Pass a path on the left but continue straight then curve left across the bridge. The creek is about 25 feet wide and 2 feet deep, though the width and depth can vary dramatically during the year depending on the amount of rainfall. At the end of the bridge there is a mowed area and a small wetlands on the right, and hardwood trees, including oak and maple, on the left. In the spring listen for birds, frogs, and other animals in the wetlands. Follow the asphalt trail as it makes a hard right and passes some picnic tables on the left.

Commercial buildings in a retail strip can be seen to the right, on the other side of the swamp. The creek is on the left, about 5 feet away, down a small slope. A short wood fence blocks access to the creek. This section of the trail has very little tree cover to furnish shade.

The creek and woods are ideal habitat for birds and other wildlife—it is like an oasis amid the desert of the city. Look for the belted kingfisher perched in a tree

This very large crawdad was seen at the edge of the pond at Aspen Grove.

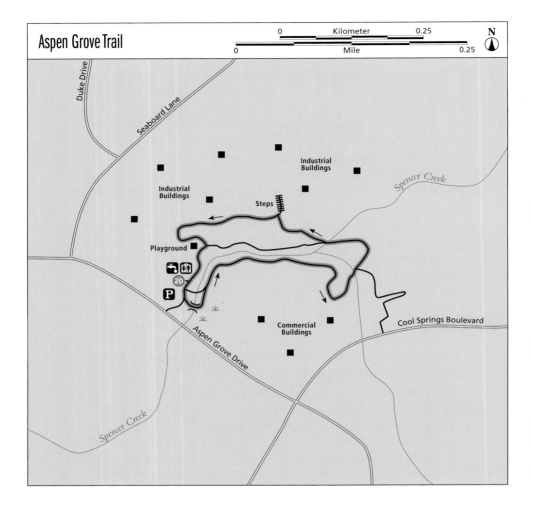

Aspen Grove Trail

Kilometer
0   0.25

Mile
0   0.25

N

Duke Drive

Seaboard Lane

Spencer Creek

Industrial
Buildings

Industrial
Buildings

Steps

Playground

20

P

Commercial
Buildings

Cool Springs Boulevard

Aspen Grove Drive

Spencer Creek

along the creek, searching for its next meal swimming in the water. The kingfisher, about 1 foot long, is easily recognized by its conspicuous blue head and wings, slate blue breast band, and white body. Its call sounds like a loud, dry rattle. They are interesting to watch as they dive toward the water, trying to spear their next meal.

Follow the asphalt trail, heading generally east. Pass another wood fence on the left, preventing access to the creek. The creek comes in and out of view on the left. Bear hard left, away from the shopping mall and into the woods, which contains some trees as tall as 80 feet. Continue bearing left and cross a bridge over the creek. Notice the large vines, including wild grape, growing to the tops of some of the trees. Bear left as the trail forms a semicircle, which contains a bench at the midpoint. The trail weaves right and left as it follows along the creek and through the woods.

In a short distance cross a bridge and almost immediately reach a Y. Bear right, still heading generally west. Notice the bluebird nest boxes attached to posts and trees. The creek is about 4 feet away, with a 7-foot drop to it. Bear left into open canopy and at the Y take the left branch. The right branch leads to corporate offices, a reminder that this is an in-city hike. Reach a Y just past the playground, and take the right branch, which brings you back to the asphalt trail that will return you to the parking area.

MILES AND DIRECTIONS

0.0 Start at the unmarked Aspen Grove Trail trailhead adjacent to the east side of the parking area. Head east on the asphalt trail. Within the first 100 feet reach a T, with a shelter and playground on the left, and take the right branch toward a bridge. Pass a path on the left and continue straight.

0.1 Curve left to a bridge over Spencer Creek, heading east. At the end of the bridge, follow the trail to the left (north), passing a small wetlands on the right.

0.2 The trail takes a hard right, following the creek about 5 feet away on the left. A commercial building and a shopping mall sit across the wetlands.

0.4 Follow the trail onto another hard right, walking toward the mall.

0.5 Cross a bridge. The trail circles around to the left, now heading northeast into the woods. The creek is on the left but cannot be seen.

0.65 Reach a Y—the left branch leads to the shelter and parking area straight ahead. Take the right branch.

0.75 Reach another Y and take the left branch, heading west. The right branch goes up steps to an office building.

0.9 Follow the trail as it makes a hard leftward loop, going south then east.

1.0 Arrive at the playground on the right. At the Y take take a sharp right to the southwest.

1.1 Reach a path to the right. Backtrack on this portion of the trail to the trailhead. End the hike at the trailhead.

Brentwood Greenway: River Park Trail

This in-city hike offers a variety of changing scenes to pique your interest. Cross over wooden bridges and follow the Little Harpeth River, with its shallow, crystal clear water and gurgling rapids. Sometimes woods and wild honeysuckle edge the trail; other times, soccer fields or tennis courts. This is an excellent hike for families with young children.

Start: At the unmarked River Park Trail trailhead at the northeast side of the parking area
Distance: 2.7 miles out and back
Approximate hiking time: 1.5 hours
Difficulty: Easy due to flat paved trail
Trail surface: Asphalt
Best season: September to June
Other trail users: Joggers, bicyclists, skateboarders, dog walkers, strollers, wheelchairs
Canine compatibility: Leashed dogs permitted

Fees and permits: None required
Schedule: Dawn to dusk
Maps: USGS: Franklin
Trail contact: Brentwood Parks and Recreation Department, 1750 General George Patton Dr., Brentwood, TN 37027; (615) 371-0080; www.brentwood-tn.org
Other: Water and restrooms are available near the parking area. There is no potable water or restrooms on the trail. Take adequate water, use insect repellant and sunscreen, and wear a hat.

Finding the trailhead: From the south side of Nashville, take I-40 East via the ramp on the left toward Knoxville and go 0.9 mile. Merge onto I-65 South via exit 210 toward Huntsville and go 10.9 miles. Take TN 253, exit 71, toward Brentwood and go 0.4 mile. Turn left onto Concord Road and go 0.6 mile, then turn right onto Knox Valley Drive and proceed 0.2 mile to 1200 Knox Valley Dr. in Brentwood. Follow the park road to the parking area and trailhead. *DeLorme Tennessee Atlas & Gazetteer:* Page 53, D5. GPS: N35 59.70' / W86 47.25'

T his out-and-back trail is located in Brentwood's River Park and is part of the Brentwood Greenway system. The outbound section heads south, with the inbound returning north. Stay on the right side of this wide, multiuse, and paved trail to give other users the opportunity to pass. Always give notice when passing people (on the left) who are using strollers or wheelchairs. Benches are conveniently placed along the trail, which is well signed with markers.

Brentwood has created a boon for hikers by connecting and routing trails along creeks and floodplains that normally would be considered unusable. An example is this hike, which parallels the Little Harpeth River and its floodplain. Crockett Park, another component of the greenway, can be reached via a tunnel under Wilson Pike and the CSX railroad tracks. This hike and Crockett Park may represent the in-city hiking of the future. Water fountains, restrooms, a playground, a shelter, and picnic tables are adjacent to the parking area. These can be an incentive to hikers with young children.

Begin your hike at the unmarked River Park Trail trailhead at the east side of the parking area. Pass a sign that reads ENTERING RIVER PARK BIKEWAY, then immediately cross a bridge over the Little Harpeth River and turn right, heading south. There is a large map board at the end of the bridge. If you plan to alter your hike, study the

The Little Harpeth River borders much of the River Park Trail.

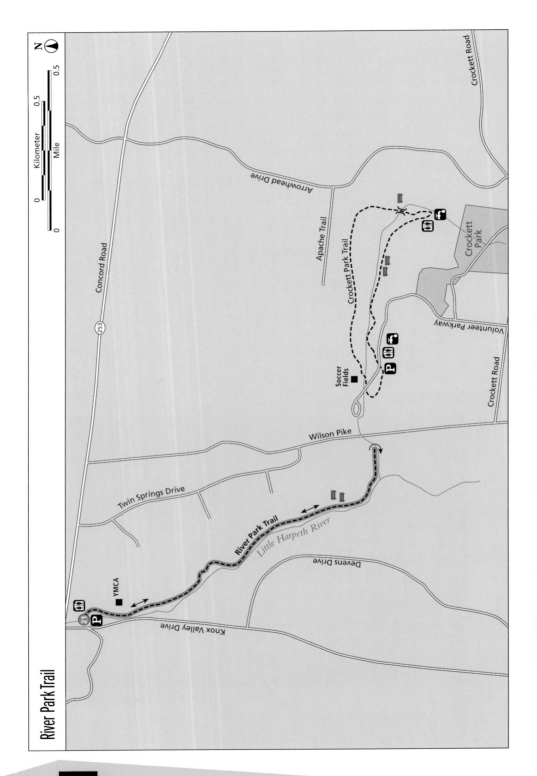

River Park Trail

map. The Brentwood YMCA and soccer fields are to the left. Continue following the trail along the river, which is on the right. Mowed grass is on each side of the trail, along with woods on the right. Pass several concrete picnic tables on the right, with the river behind them about 20 feet away. Follow the trail as it bears hard left, still heading generally south. Three-rail wood fences are on the left.

The trail bends right and then reaches a walk-around containing a picnic table. Continue left around the picnic table. The river is on the right but cannot be seen. Pass a two-bench shelter (a small covered shelter with back-to-back benches), a signature feature of this park. At marker post 3, bear right, then hard left, still heading generally south. Notice the fence on the left, enclosing a horse pasture—Tennesseans love their horses. There is a small clearing on the right, and the river can be seen about 25 feet away. A large group of limestone blocks is scattered in the clearing on the right. Follow the trail as it gets within 6 feet of the river. This is a very picturesque section, creating a great opportunity for photos.

Reach a short loop around a two-sided covered shelter. Take either branch, since they rejoin after the shelter. Within 250 feet reach a bench at the river's edge, facing the water. Honeysuckle bushes and large sycamore trees, which can grow 10 feet a year, line the river's edge. A sign behind the bench gives information about the Little Harpeth River, noting that the Little Harpeth feeds the Harpeth. In the spring and early summer, black-eyed Susans, Queen Anne's lace, and orange-flowering trumpet vines are all in vibrant bloom. Return to the trail and while heading south, pass a lighted emergency call box. Pass marker post 6 while continuing south.

Catch a glimpse of the river, about 10 feet away, as it bends. Hardwood trees line the river bank. Follow the trail as it bends left and pass marker post 7. As the trail draws closer to the river, listen for the soft gurgling of rapids. The level and flow of the river can vary greatly depending on the amount of rainfall. The tree canopy is open, affording little shade. Listen for birds while passing marker post 8, especially the eastern phoebe. This 7-inch-long bird is easily identified by its distinctive song, a harsh emphatic *fee-bee*. It is brownish gray on its upper body and white on its belly.

Pass marker post 9 and a two-bench covered shelter, and continue following the trail as it bends right and reaches a T. Take the left branch, still heading generally south. The right branch leads to Wikle Road. Continue following the asphalt trail until reaching a marker that states Turn Around. Just ahead is the tunnel under Wilson Pike and the CSX railroad tracks that leads to Crockett Park. This is a good spot to turn around and backtrack to the trailhead.

> **Green Tip:**
> *Pack out your dog's waste or dispose of it
> in a trash can or a hole dug into the ground.*

0.0 Start at the unmarked River Park Trail trailhead at the northeast edge of the parking area.

0.1 Immediately cross a bridge over the Little Harpeth River and turn right, heading south. There is a large map board at the end of the bridge. The Brentwood YMCA and soccer fields are to the left. Continue following the trail along the river, which is on the right.

0.3 Reach a circular walk-around with a picnic table in the center. Follow to the left, still heading generally south.

0.3 Pass several trail marker posts and a three-rail wood pasture fence on the left. Bear left; the river is about 8 feet away on the right.

0.5 Continue following the trail generally south and reach a narrow Y. The left and right branches form a loop around a shelter that has a bench. Follow either branch, since they meet and rejoin the trail. The river is on the right, and some residences can be seen on the left. Pass a bench on the right and a sign describing the Little Harpeth River.

0.7 Pass an emergency call box on the left, which is lighted at night. Continue generally south and pass marker posts 6 and 7. Bend left, temporarily heading west. The river is about 10 feet away on the right. Pass marker post 8.

0.9 Cross a drainage culvert and bear left and then right, passing a path leading to the river, which is about 50 feet away. Pass marker post 9 and a covered shelter on the left.

1.0 Continue following the trail as it gets nearer the river. Small rapids may be heard. The trail bends right and reaches a T. Take the left branch along the Little Harpeth River, heading southeast. The right branch leads to Wikle Road.

1.2 Reach a Y and take the left branch. The right branch is a path to Ravenwood High School.

1.35 Bear left toward the Wilson Pike and railroad underpass. Reach a marker on the right that says, TURN AROUND. Continue on to investigate the underpass and then backtrack to the trailhead.

2.7 End the hike at the trailhead.

Brentwood Greenway: Crockett Park Trail

This hike offers woods, a meandering stream, bridges, and open areas to hold your interest. Several wooden bridges span meanders of the Little Harpeth River and lead to woods or open clearings. Tall hardwood trees, including oak and maple edge the trail. Covered benches are placed conveniently along the route.

Start: Unmarked Crockett Park Trail trailhead at the north side of the parking area
Distance: 1.8-mile counterclockwise loop
Approximate hiking time: 1 hour
Difficulty: East due to flat paved surface
Trail surface: Asphalt
Best season: September to June
Other trail users: Joggers, bicyclists, skateboarders, dog walkers, strollers, wheelchairs
Canine compatibility: Leashed dogs allowed

Fees and permits: None required
Schedule: 8:00 a.m. to 10:00 p.m.
Maps: USGS: Franklin; map boards along the trail
Trail contact: Brentwood Parks and Recreation Department, 1750 General George Patton Dr., Brentwood, TN 37027; (615) 371-0080; www.brentwood-tn.org
Other: Water fountains and restrooms are located adjacent to the parking area and at 0.9 mile. Use insect repellant and sunscreen and wear a hat.

Finding the trailhead: From the south side of Nashville, take I-40 East via the ramp on the left toward Knoxville and go 0.9 mile. Merge onto I-65 South, exit 210, toward Huntsville and go 10.9 miles. Take TN 253, exit 71, toward Brentwood and go 0.4 mile. Turn left onto Concord Road and go 1.1 miles, then turn right onto Wilson Pike and go 1.3 mile. Turn left onto Crockett Road and go 0.3 mile, then turn left onto Volunteer Parkway and go 0.3 mile to 1500 Volunteer Pkwy. in Brentwood. Follow the park road to the parking area and trailhead. *DeLorme Tennessee Atlas & Gazetteer:* Page 53, D5. GPS: N35 58.98' / W86 46.35'

This wide, multiuse, paved trail is located in Brentwood's Crockett Park and is part of the Brentwood Greenway system. Stay on the right side of the trail to give other users the opportunity to pass. Always give notice when passing people (on the left) using strollers or wheelchairs. Covered benches are conveniently placed along the trail, which is well signed with markers.

Brentwood has created a boon for hikers by connecting and routing trails along creeks and floodplains that normally would be considered unusable land. River Park, another section of the greenway, can be reached via a tunnel under Wilson Pike and the CSX railroad tracks. This hike and the River Park hike may rep-

This interesting underpass connects the trails from Crockett Park and River Park.

resent the in-city hiking of the future. Amenities, including water fountains, rest-rooms, a playground, a pavilion, and picnic tables, are adjacent to the parking area. These can be an incentive to hikers with young children.

From the unmarked Crockett Park Trail trailhead at the northeast side of the parking area, go less than 25 feet north and turn right, heading east, at a green marker post. A meander of the Little Harpeth River and some trees are on the left, and the parking area is on the right. There is mowed grass along both sides of the trail. Watch for squirrels, rabbits, and birds. Many of them have lost most of their fear of humans, allowing for good pictures. Pass a black marker post on the left; the river is on the right, about 8 feet away. Good tree canopy furnishes shade along this part of the trail. Cross a bridge over the river and a bench on the left; turn right and continue past a path that comes in from the right. Trees arch over and above the trail, forming a tunnel.

Continue heading generally south to a T. Take the right branch, heading toward a shelter, and almost immediately reach a Y. Take the left branch, heading away from the shelter. The grass near the trail is mowed, and there are hardwood trees, including oak and maple. Reach a two-bench shelter. These shelters with back-to-back benches are a signature feature of the park and were constructed by Eagle Scouts of Troop 418. Head down slightly as the trail squiggles left, right, and back left, still going generally south. Bear right and pass marker post 13. (The marker posts will not be in strict order, due to the particular section of trail chosen for this hike.) Look for honeysuckle blooming in the spring.

Pass a bench on the right and immediately cross a bridge over the river. Within 25 feet reach a Y and take the left branch, leading to a mowed field. Pass marker post 15 and bear left, and continue bearing left as the trail forms a semicircle. Pass a covered bench and leave the mowed clearing, heading into the woods. Many birds call these woods home, including the downy woodpecker. This small bird, only 7 inches long, with white on its back and cheeks, black wings, and a red spot on its head, is somewhat unwary, allowing for observation at fairly close range. Bear left and right through the woods while passing marker post 3.

Reach a Y with restrooms and a water fountain on the right. Take the right branch, heading north. The left branch leads back to the shelter. In a short distance make a hard left, heading west. The left side of the trail is mowed grass, and the right side is soccer field 6. Pass marker post 4 on the right and a bridge on the left. Soccer field 5 is on the right, and a two-bench covered shelter, overlooking the river, is on the left. Continue west and pass soccer fields 4, 3, 2, and 1, which adjoin each other, and then go by the fenced tennis courts, picnic tables, and a water fountain.

In a very short distance reach a Y and take the right branch. This is a short out and back to view the tunnel under Wilson Pike and the CSX railroad tracks that leads to River Park. Return to the Y and take the right branch, which leads back to the trailhead and parking area.

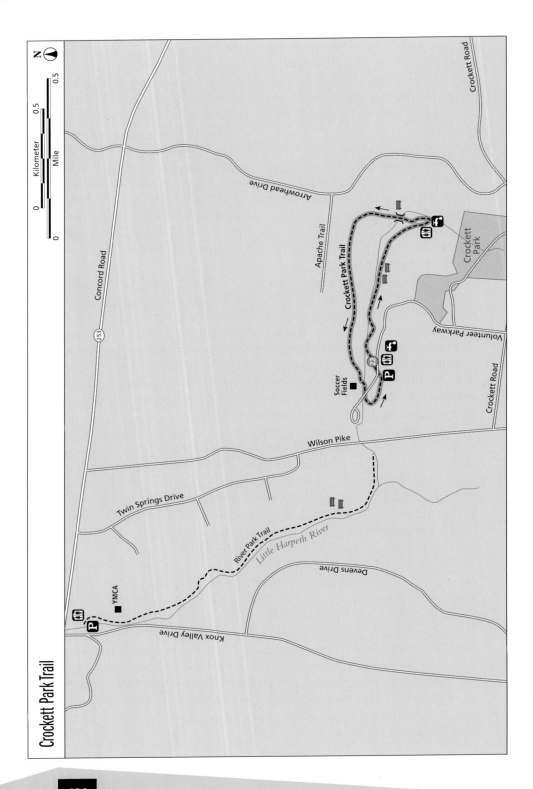

0.0   Start at the unmarked Crockett Park Trail trailhead at the north side of the paved parking area. This trail is well signed.

0.1   Head north for less than 100 feet on the paved surface and cross a bridge. At the end of the bridge, turn right, bearing slightly left and down. Continue following the asphalt trail east.

0.3   Reach a T and take the right branch, heading north for a short distance, then follow the trail to the left, now heading east. A picnic shelter is on the right. Almost immediately reach a Y and take the left branch, heading north, then bear right, heading east. Pass a two-bench covered shelter and continue following the trail.

0.5   Weave through woods and open areas until reaching a Y; take the left branch, still heading generally east. Follow the trail left and slightly down.

0.6   Continue following the trail generally east and cross a bridge. Take a hard right at the end of the bridge and head south. Almost immediately reach a Y and take the left branch. Bear left as the trail forms a semicircle and passes a covered bench. Continue following the trail in a generally south direction.

0.9   Pass a two-bench covered shelter as the trail veers left and right, heading generally south. Reach concrete block restrooms and water fountains. At the Y just beyond the restrooms, take the right branch as it follows around and heads north. The left branch crosses a bridge and returns to the shelter, shortening the hike.

1.2   Follow the trail north as it veers right and left, then make a hard left, heading west. Pass several soccer fields on the right and a bench and continue following the asphalt trail generally west. The river is on the left.

1.4   Pass a bridge on the left and soccer field 1 on the right. Reach a Y and take the right branch, which follows along the soccer fields. Continue heading west past fenced tennis courts. Water and picnic tables are available. Reach a Y and take the right branch, then follow the trail until reaching the tunnel under the CSX tracks and Wilson Pike. The path through the tunnel leads to River Park. Backtrack to the parking area.

1.8   End the hike at the parking area.

Land Trust for Tennessee

Tennessee, as most states, has been losing significant portions of property to real estate developers and the growth of cities. Historic sites and landscapes as well as unique natural areas, have fallen to the bulldozer creating shopping malls and new residential communities. While important to growth, this development precludes these historic and natural features from being enjoyed by future generations.

The Land Trust for Tennessee, a 501(c)(3) nonprofit organization, was established in 1999 to help stem this tide. The group works exclusively with willing landowners to find ways to preserve forever the scenic and natural values of their land. Their main tool is called a "conservation easement." This tool gives the landowner another option than selling his land for development. The landowner receives three important benefits: 1) he/(she) continues to own the land; 2) the important natural assets of the property are preserved through the use of customized restrictions on the future use of the land; and 3) certain tax advantages are available to some of these property owners. These are powerful incentives to encourage them to enter into the agreement.

Folks at The Land Trust spend much time in the field, evaluating and investigating potential sites. After a landowner has contacted The Land Trust, staff members will visit the property to determine if the site has the conservation values necessary to preserve their land. Upon determining that a property does have conservation value, Land Trust staff work with landowners and their legal counsel to develop the best future use of the property. Countless hours of behind-the-scenes legal work are going on continuously. The final agreement is a win-win situation for the landowner and future generations that will have the opportunity to enjoy these natural areas. Although the majority of The Land Trust's protected lands are privately owned, a number of sites are now available for viewing and hiking.

The staff at The Land Trust for Tennessee invites you to visit and enjoy the low-impact activities at the following protected landscapes that are open to the public:

- Roper's Knob (Williamson County)
- Harlinsdale Farm (Williamson County)
- Franklin Battlefield at Carnton (Williamson County) (hike 18)
- Stones River Road (Davidson County)—not yet open, but will be the trailhead to Stones River Greenway
- Bowie Park (Williamson County) (hike 31)
- The Hill Tract at Warner Parks (Davidson County)—new hiking rails are not yet open

This may be the most interesting hike in this guide. It starts out in typical karst topography, with limestone outcrops and sinkholes, and passes a stone wall about 600 feet long and of undetermined origin. The trail weaves through limestone blocks and then reaches the West Fork of the Stones River, where an overlook provides views of the rapids.

Start: Connector trail next to the Wilderness Station leading to the Wilderness Trail
Distance: 2.7-mile clockwise loop
Approximate hiking time: 2 hours to allow time at the river
Difficulty: Moderate due to limestone outcrops and elevation changes
Trail surface: Dirt, rock, asphalt
Best season: Year-round
Other trail users: Dog walkers
Canine compatibility: Leashed dogs permitted
Fees and permits: None required
Schedule: 8:00 a.m. to 8:00 p.m.
Maps: USGS: Murfreesboro; trail maps and brochures available at the Wilderness Station
Trail contact: Manager, Barfield Crescent Park, Wilderness Station, 697 Barfield Crescent Rd., Murfreesboro, TN 37128; (615) 217-3017; www.murfreesborotn .gov/parks
Other: Water and restrooms are available at the Wilderness Station and the campground. Take water and use insect repellant. If hiking with young children, keep them on the trail and close to you, since some of the sinkholes are at the edge of the trail.

Finding the trailhead: From the east side of Nashville, take I-40 East toward Knoxville for 4.0 miles. Keep right to take I-24 East via exit 213A, toward Chattanooga for 29.6 miles. Then merge onto South Church Street/US 231S/TN10S and continue for 2.2 miles to exit 81A toward Shelbyville. Turn right onto Barfield Crescent Road and continue for 0.9 mile until reaching 697 Barfield Crescent Road. Turn left into the park entrance and follow the park road to the Wilderness Station. *DeLorme Tennessee Atlas & Gazetteer:* Page 38, B1. GPS: N35 46.53' / W86 24.78'

Pick up a trail map and interpretive brochure at the Wilderness Station before starting your hike at the Wilderness Trail trailhead, behind the station. The trail follows a clockwise loop over karst terrain and through the woods. Near the end of the trail, there is short section of paved asphalt that may be used by those pushing strollers or using wheelchairs.

Head south into the woods and follow the short (0.3-mile) connector to the beginning of the Wilderness Trail. The ground surface furnishes excellent examples of karst topography. A karst is an area underlaid with limestone and having limestone outcrops on the surface. Limestone is a soft porous rock, and water seeping through it forms caves and underground rivers. Over time some of the caves collapse, forming sinkholes and crevasses. Middle Tennessee has the largest karst area in the country. The surface limestone can form walls and other interesting formations, furnishing some great photo ops.

Red blazes painted on the trees identify the trail. Look for limestone, which is normally gray or black, to have some streaks of red. Limestone outcrops 2 to 3 feet high reach to the trail's edge. Weave back and forth, heading up through the woods. Sugar maple, various oak species, shagbark hickory, and cedar are among

A hiker explores one of the crevasses on the Wilderness Trail in Barfield Crescent Park.

the many varieties of trees. The uphill slopes are generally not steep. Birds can be heard, but are difficult to see in the woods.

Cross a boardwalk over a wet area and pass the remnants of an old rusted fence. This is a good spot to look for grasses and ferns, including bunches of big bluestone grass and rattlesnake fern. Sinkholes and limestone outcrops continue to be the rule of the day. Many of the sinkholes are around 8 feet wide, 7 feet deep, and 30 feet long. Use caution when near these. Continue watching for the red blazes as the trail zigzags back and forth, sometimes making hard right and left turns, in a short distance.

As the Wilderness Trail begins to flatten, look ahead for the nearly intact remains of a stone wall. Bear hard left and follow along the wall. In the spring wildflowers grow along and out of it. The wall continues for 600 feet, and there are opportunities to go up to it and investigate. This area is at the top of the hill and overlooks Murfreesboro and the Stones River. Confederate General Braxton Bragg camped here for several days prior to the Battle of Murfreesboro. There has been much conjecture about the origin of the wall. Some Civil War experts feel the general had the wall built when he camped here. This is a great place to rest and use your imagination before turning left at the end of the wall and heading slightly down.

Reach a T, with a deep sinkhole to its left. Take the right branch and continue following the red blazes marking the Wilderness Trail. (The left branch is the Valley View Trail and is identified by a blue blaze.) You are now nearly a mile from the Wilderness Station. Pass a bench and make a hard left, heading down, then cross over a gravel road that leads to the campground. Bear right as the trail narrows and parallels the park boundary fence. Try to identify some of the trees, which include flowering dogwood, with its delicate white blooms in the spring.

The trail follows the West Fork of the Stones River, which can barely be seen. Look for catalpa trees in the woods. These trees grow tall and have long seed pods in the fall. Cross a short bridge over a gully, with the fence now out of view. Pass a bench on the right, overlooking the river, which is about 30 feet away. Skirt by the campground, which offers restrooms and water, on the right and up in the woods. Upon reaching the river, take a short out and back to the river overlook to explore the rapids before returning to the trail. Head up the trail, noticing signs that identify various trees, including red oak and butternut hickory. Reach a Y and take the left branch to head back to the Wilderness Station and trailhead.

🌿 Green Tip:
Consider citronella as an effective natural mosquito repellent.

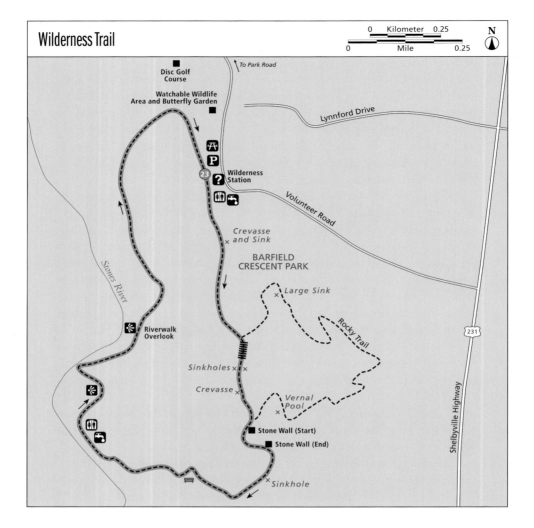

Wilderness Trail

0   Kilometer   0.25

0   Mile   0.25

N

To Park Road

Disc Golf Course

Watchable Wildlife Area and Butterfly Garden

Lynnford Drive

Wilderness Station

Volunteer Road

Crevasse and Sink

BARFIELD CRESCENT PARK

Large Sink

Rocky Trail

Stones River

Riverwalk Overlook

Sinkholes

Crevasse

Vernal Pool

Stone Wall (Start)

Stone Wall (End)

Shelbyville Highway

231

Sinkhole

MILES AND DIRECTIONS

0.0   Start at the Wilderness Trail connector trail behind the Wilderness Station. The trail is a clockwise loop heading generally south, west, and north, and is marked by red blazes on trees.

0.1   Pass many limestone outcrops and crevasses, taking time to explore a crevasse on the right that is about 4 feet wide, 50 feet long, and 10 feet deep. Use caution. Return to the trail, turning right and heading south.

0.3   At this point, reach the Wilderness Trail. Follow the trail as it weaves through the woods and limestone outcrops. Pass a large oak tree on the left with a 30-inch diameter. Pass a bench on the left and cross a boardwalk going over a wet area.

0.5 Follow the red-blazed trail as it veers right, left, and back right. Pass a large sinkhole on the left, then make a hard right and immediate hard left, going up between rocks. Use caution, as some sinkholes are at the trail's edge.

0.6 Pass a sign that states it is 0.6 mile back to Wilderness Station. Reach the start of a stone wall about 4 feet high and 600 feet long. The trail follows the wall, which is on the left about 10 feet away.

0.8 Reach a T with a sinkhole to the left. Take the right branch (the red-blazed trail) and continue heading generally south. The left branch is the blue-blazed Valley View Trail.

0.9 Reach another T and take the right branch.

1.0 Continue until reaching another T. Take the right branch, which is relatively flat. Bear right, heading northwest.

1.1 Reach a gravel road and cross it to a path that leads to a T at the park boundary fence. Take the right branch, noting the red blaze painted on a tree.

1.2 Follow the trail as it makes a hard right, heading north, with the West Fork of the Stones River on the left, about 30 feet away.

1.6 Follow along the river as it comes in and out of view while the trail weaves back and forth and up and down. Cross a short bridge over a gully and pass along the campground on the right.

1.8 Reach the river, where a short path to the left leads to the rapids and an overlook. Follow right and up a slope until the dirt trail changes to asphalt. This is the Virtual Tree Trail.

2.0 Continue on the asphalt trail, going slightly up until reaching a Y. Take the left branch toward the Wilderness Station. The right branch leads to the campground. This is still part of the Virtual Tree Trail. Follow the asphalt trail as it slopes up.

2.3 Pass several benches and more trees identified on the Virtual Tree Trail. Follow the asphalt trail as it continues to slope up.

2.4 Reach a Y and take the right branch that leads to the Wilderness Station. The trail begins to flatten, and woods are to the right and left.

2.7 End the hike at the Wilderness Station.

Barfield Crescent Park: Rocky Trail

This single-track trail leads through rugged karst topography with limestone out-crops and boulders, crevasses, and large sinkholes. Large blocks of limestone make up part of the trail. A vernal pool is nearly hidden in the woods, and wildflowers and birds are abundant in the springtime. This may be the most difficult hike in this guide, but it's well worth the effort.

Start: Connector trail next to the Wilderness Station leading to the Rocky Trail trailhead
Distance: 2.5-mile lollipop
Approximate hiking time: 2 hours
Difficulty: Difficult due to rocky outcrops and moderate inclines
Trail surface: Dirt, rock
Best season: Year-round
Other trail users: Dog walkers
Canine compatibility: Leashed dogs permitted
Fees and permits: None required
Schedule: 8:00 a.m. to 8:00 p.m.
Maps: USGS: Murfreesboro; trail maps and brochures available at the Wilderness Station
Trail contact: Manager, Barfield Crescent Park, Wilderness Station, 697 Barfield Crescent Rd., Murfreesboro, TN 37128; (615) 217-3017; www.murfreesborotn.gov/parks
Other: Water and restrooms are available at the Wilderness Station and campground. There is no potable water or restrooms on the trail. Take adequate water, use sunscreen and insect repellant, and wear a hat.

Finding the trailhead: From the east side of Nashville, take I-40 East toward Knoxville for 4.0 miles. Keep right to take I-24 East via exit 213A, toward Chattanooga for 29.6 miles. Then merge onto South Church Street/US 231S/TN10S and continue for 2.2 miles to exit 81A toward Shelbyville. Turn right onto Barfield Crescent Road and continue for 0.9 mile until reaching 697 Barfield Crescent Road. Turn left into the park entrance and follow the park road to the Wilderness Station. *DeLorme Tennessee Atlas & Gazetteer:* Page 38, B1. GPS: N35 46.56' / W86 24.80'

THE HIKE

he Rocky Trail is located in the 275-acre backcountry section that has been added to Barfield Crescent Park in Murfreesboro. Constructed and maintained by the Tennessee Trails Association, this rugged 2.5-mile lollipop hike with a clockwise loop is the most difficult hike in this guide and is not recommended for young children.

The ground surface furnishes excellent examples of karst outcrops. A karst is an area underlaid with limestone and having limestone outcrops on the surface. Limestone is a soft porous rock, and water seeping through it forms caves and underground rivers. Over time some of the caves collapse, forming sinkholes and crevasses. The surface limestone can form walls and other interesting formations, including individual blocks of limestone, furnishing some great photo ops. Middle Tennessee has the largest karst area in the country. The trail leads through hardwood forests, weaving past a vernal pond and around limestone outcrops, crevasses, and major sinkholes while crossing Marshall's Knobs.

Pick up a trail map and interpretive brochure at the Wilderness Station before your hike. Start at the Rocky Trail connector trail behind the station. Head south into the woods and follow the short (0.3-mile) connector to the beginning of the

A vernal pool along the Rocky Trail in Barfield Crescent Park can only be seen after a spring rainfall.

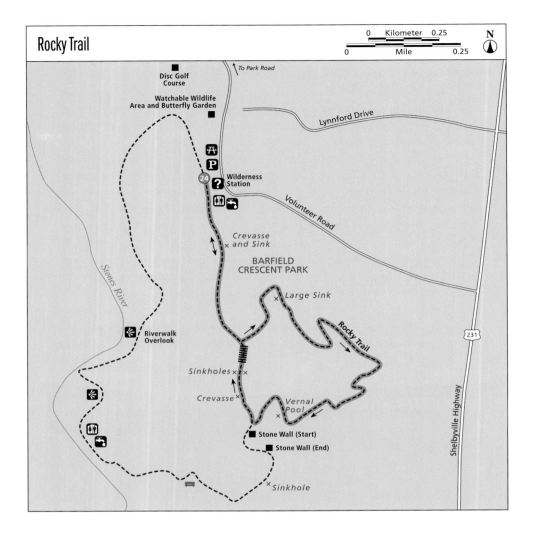

0 Kilometer 0.25

0 Mile 0.25

N

To Park Road

Disc Golf
Course

Watchable Wildlife
Area and Butterfly Garden

Lynnford Drive

24

Wilderness
Station

Volunteer Road

Crevasse
× and Sink

BARFIELD
CRESCENT PARK

Stones River

× Large Sink

Rocky Trail

231

Riverwalk
Overlook

Sinkholes × × ×

Crevasse ×

Vernal
Pool
×

Stone Wall (Start)

Stone Wall (End)

Shelbyville Highway

× Sinkhole

Rocky Trail. The connector trail also services the Wilderness Trail, identified by red blazes. Reach a Y and take the left branch onto the Rocky Trail and head south. Veer left and right around limestone outcrops while heading slightly uphill, with the trail identified by white blazes. The trail narrows while passing a gully and then leads up a few limestone steps.

Continue heading southeast while passing large pieces of limestone and sinkholes. Some of the sinkholes can be up to 150 feet long, 35 feet across, and 12 feet deep. This is the finest example of karst topography in middle Tennessee. Pass a bench on the right, offering a shady rest spot. Continue bearing left and right and reach a sharp left turn in the trail, between 0.7 and 0.8 mile into the hike. This turn is not well marked and the white blazes seem to disappear. The trail actually doubles back on itself, separated by a crevasse. Notice the line of rectangular blocks of limestone to the north, each about 2 feet wide, 3 feet long, and 2 feet high and a foot or two apart. Five or six of them can be investigated. Use extreme caution if trying to walk across them, since a fall can result in a broken bone.

In a short distance turn right, heading southwest. Some pieces of limestone must be straddled to continue on the trail. Look into the woods and try to identify the trees that include sugar maple, eastern hophornbeam, cedar, and hackberry. The eastern hophornbeam can be identified by its light brown bark and shaggy appearance. It is said that the wood of this tree is so hard that the Romans used it to build chariots. Look for clumps of bluestem grass, which is also called turkey foot because its flowering stem resembles the foot of a turkey. It's a grass native to this area and attracts birds and rodents. Shaded areas support communities of both the walking fern and resurrection fern.

Follow the trail, with its white blazes, as it bears west, sometimes finding it necessary to skirt around limestone outcrops or step up and down 12 to 18 inches. The trail continues to zigzag until reaching a path on the left that leads to a shallow vernal pool about 25 feet away, almost hidden by the woods. Take a short out and back to investigate the pool and its amphibian residents. Return to the trail and turn right, going a short distance north, and then turn left, heading south and then bearing west. In a very short distance make a hard right, heading north, until reaching a T. Take the right branch onto the red-blazed Wilderness Trail, still heading north. Follow the trail until reaching a Y and take the left branch, staying on the Wilderness Trail and backtracking to the Wilderness Station. The Rocky Trail has certainly earned its name!

MILES AND DIRECTIONS

0.0   Start at the connector trail behind the Wilderness Station that leads to the Rocky Trail.

0.1   Veer left and right into the woods on the trail, which is also part of the Wilderness Trail, identified by red blazes painted on trees. Pass a sinkhole on the right edge of the trail, then reach another sinkhole and crevasse and bear right, heading south. Continue following the narrow trail over limestone outcrops between the trees.

0.3   Reach a Y and take the left branch onto the Rocky Trail, heading east and then south. The Rocky Trail is identified by white blazes painted on trees. The trail leads up several limestone steps. Take a hard left at the next white blaze, still heading generally south.

0.5 Follow the white blazes and pass a large sinkhole, then pass a bench on the right. Continue following the trail in a generally south direction as it zigzags.

0.7 The trail bears hard left, doubling back on itself and heading slightly down. This section is opposite the trail just hiked.

0.8 Pass a white blaze and make a hard right, doubling back on the trail. The trail weaves through the trees and the limestone outcrops, heading generally southeast.

1.0 Pass a bench and bear hard right, heading southwest. Continue following the trail southwest as it zigzags. This is a long section with few distinguishing features.

1.8 Make a hard right and reach a path on the left leading to a vernal pool. Investigate the pool and return to the trail, heading north for a short distance, then bear hard left for a short distance, heading south.

2.0 Follow the trail as it angles southwest a short distance and then bear hard right, heading north.

2.2 Reach the Y at the connector trail and take the left branch, heading north toward the Wilderness Station.

2.5 End the hike at the Wilderness Station.

Murfreesboro Greenway: Cason Trail

This paved trail follows the West Fork of the Stones River, which comes in and out of view. Great views of the river can be had from the 500-foot-long pedestrian bridge. The length of the bridge is awesome and a high point of the hike. This linear trail in Murfreesboro is part of the city's greenway system.

Start: Cason Trail trailhead adjacent to the parking area
Distance: 2 miles out and back
Approximate hiking time: 1 hour
Difficulty: Easy due to flat, wide, paved trail
Trail surface: Asphalt
Best season: Year-round
Other trail users: Joggers, inline skaters, bicyclists, wheelchairs, strollers, dog walkers
Canine compatibility: Leashed dogs permitted
Fees and permits: None required
Schedule: Dawn to one hour before dusk

Maps: USGS: Murfreesboro; large mounted trail map near each trailhead
Trail contact: Murfreesboro Greenway System, 697 Barfield Crescent Road, Murfreesboro, TN 37128; (615) 890-5333; www.murfreesborotn.gov
Other: Restrooms and water fountains are available at the trailhead. There is no potable water or restrooms on the trail. Take adequate water, use insect repellant and sunscreen, and wear a hat.

Finding the trailhead: From the east side of Nashville, take I-40 East via the ramp on the left toward Knoxville go 4 miles. Keep right to take I-24 East, exit 213A, toward Chattanooga and go 26.4 miles. Merge onto Old Fort Parkway, exit 78A, toward Franklin and go 0.4 mile. Turn left onto Cason Trail and go 1.1 miles to 1100 Cason Trail, Murfreesboro, on the right. Proceed to the parking area and trailhead. *DeLorme Tennessee Atlas & Gazetteer:* Page 38, A2. GPS: N35 49.53' / W86 25.45'

25

THE HIKE

Murfreesboro has created a boon for hikers by connecting trails and routing them along river and creek floodplains that normally would be considered unusable. The city has built bridges over the Stones River that connect trails, and it has incorporated the Stones River National Battlefield, site of the Battle of Murfreesboro, a major Civil War battle, and the Cotton Field Trail into its greenway trail system. This type of planning and creativity may be the model for in-city hiking.

The Cason Trail is one of ten trails in the extensive Murfreesboro Greenway system. Several more trails are in the planning stage. Trails and greenways are not synonymous. A trail is a path, while a greenway is a corridor of open space. Most greenways offer public access and have trails. This 12-foot-wide multiuse paved trail is accessible to a variety of users. Stay on the right side of the trail to give other users the opportunity to pass, and always give notice when passing people (on the left) using strollers or wheelchairs. Benches are conveniently placed along the trail, and it is well signed with markers.

This 2-mile out-and-back trail heads a short distance east to the West Fork of the Stones River, then follows the river as it heads north and bends west on the

Many trails in city parks pass by playgrounds to attract young hikers.

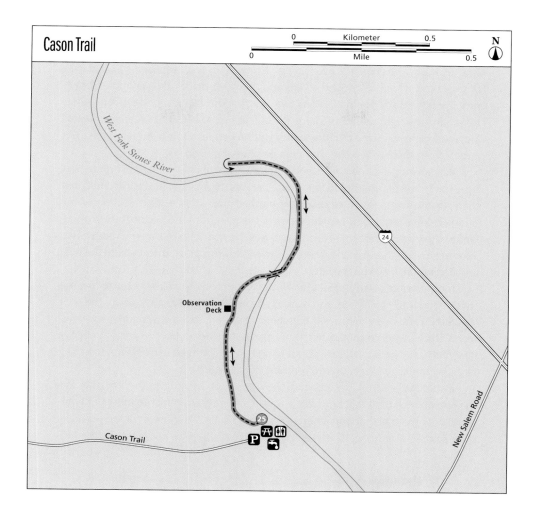

Cason Trail

outbound leg of the hike, reversing this on the inbound leg. Begin your hike at the large paved parking area off Cason Trail. The main park area is here and contains several shelters, a playground, restrooms, and water fountains. Follow around a building and head slightly down, and within 150 feet reach a T. Take the left branch and immediately reach a Y. Take the right branch and follow slightly to the right and then make a hard left, crossing a bridge over an unnamed creek. The West Fork of the Stones River can be seen to the right. Even though the trail has zigzagged, sometimes heading north for a short distance and sometimes heading east, the overall direction has been east for this short stretch.

Bear hard left, heading north with the river on the right. Follow north paralleling the river and passing some large—up to 7 feet long and 2 feet high—limestone blocks. Cross a bridge over a meander of the Stones River and continue straight, heading basically north. Follow the trail slightly up and pass a group of limestone boulders near the river's edge. A clearing in the trees allows a good view of the river. The woods contain cedars and hardwoods, including shagbark hickories. The left side of the trail is lined with grass about 30 feet to the woods, while trees edge the right side. Pass a large flat outcrop of limestone, 7 feet from the trail and extending for 50 feet. In the spring wildflowers, including daisies, carpet this area. Unfortunately, there are also large patches of poison ivy.

Bear slightly left, then right, and reach a bridge of major size. This bridge over the Stones River is about 500 feet long. It slopes slightly up, bends hard left, and then gently slopes down to reach the asphalt trail. Only a short section of the bridge crosses the river. The great views of the river from the bridge furnish excellent photo opportunities. The bridge crosses the river in an easterly direction and joins the trail on the opposite side. Continue following the trail north, with the river and a three-rail fence on the left.

In the spring white and sulphur butterflies may be seen. These butterflies are small, about half-dollar size, and congregate around puddles after a rain. The river is about 40 feet away on the left but cannot be seen. Low grasses and a few limestone blocks are also on the left, while the right side harbors a grassy meadow. Bear hard left, heading west; a billboard on I-24 can be seen over the treetops. The highway cannot be seen, but traffic noise can be heard.

Pass some vertical limestone on the left, about 5 feet from the trail, that has the appearance of an old crumbling wall. Notice a group of large pieces of limestone near the trail that appear orange-colored, which is strange for the normally slate-colored limestone. Continue west and reach a three-rail fence on the left,

Large clumps of moss can be seen along the Cason Trail, even though it's an urban trail.

with a large outcrop of limestone on the right. This is a great spot to stop and back-track to the trailhead.

MILES AND DIRECTIONS

0.0 Start at the Cason Trail trailhead adjacent to the parking area and head east toward the West Fork of the Stones River.

0.1 Within 150 feet reach a T and take the left branch, heading slightly northwest, and almost immediately reach a Y and take the right branch, heading north. Follow the trail slightly to the right and then make a hard left and cross a bridge over an unnamed creek. The West Fork of the Stones River can be seen on the right. Bear hard left at the end of the bridge, heading north.

0.2 Continue following the asphalt trail north, with the river on the right. Cross a bridge over a meander of the Stones River. Continue straight at the end of the bridge, heading north.

0.4 Bear slightly left after passing a large flat outcrop of limestone on the left. Follow the asphalt trail as it veers left and then right, reaching a major bridge (about 500 feet long) over the river. At the end of the bridge bear slightly left, heading north by northeast. The river is on the left but cannot be seen. Continue following the asphalt trail north by northeast.

0.7 Pass a three-rail fence on the left protecting a slope down toward the river. Start to bear slightly left, heading north.

0.9 Follow the trail as it bears left (west). Pass limestone blocks on the left that give the appearance of a wall. Continue bearing slightly left, heading west.

1.0 Pass a three-rail fence on the left. At the end of the fence, turn around and backtrack.

2.0 End the hike at the trailhead.

Walking over the Karst

While hiking with a friend one day, I asked him what exactly a karst was and how it got there. These were perfectly natural questions to ask, as we were near Murfreesboro in middle Tennessee, an area known for its karst topography, and my companion was a Tennessee park naturalist whose specialty was karsts. He started by telling me that karst areas cover a diagonal swath starting at the southern Kentucky border and continuing to the northern border of Georgia.

He then said I should be familiar with some of the terms. Pointing toward a sinkhole, he informed me that was really a doline. Sometime sinkholes can collapse, creating a hole or possibly an entrance to an underground cave. Sinkholes are perhaps the most widespread karst feature, while caves are the best known. Dunbar Cave (hike 36) in Clarksville is an excellent example. Next we passed a gully, which had some limestone joints filled with soil—that is a grike. There were some rounded blocks of limestone in the gully—these are called dints.

I was then informed that many caves have a variety of speleothems (rock formations). These structures include stunning examples of stalactites (which hang from the ceiling) and stalagmites (which stick up from the ground) and other awesome features of karst topography, produced by the deposits of slowly dripping calcium carbonate solutions.

And, yes, there are organisms that not only live but thrive in this underground environment. Many of the creatures living in the caves don't have eyes, so some folks call them eyeless troglodytes (cave dwellers). A number of species of karst invertebrates are listed as endangered and are found only in middle Tennessee. Many of these creatures are difficult to find due to their size—only about 2 millimeters in length.

But karsts are not only caves. The surface we were walking on had many features that indicated we were over a karst: sinkholes, blocks and walls of limestone, ravines and crevasses, and at times sparse vegetation. My friend said that underground springs located in karsts supply water to several rivers and aboveground springs.

I guess my bewildered look indicated I was getting overwhelmed with interesting facts. We had been hiking and talking for a while, yet I still didn't know how karsts were formed. He smiled and told me that a karst is formed out of soluble rocks like limestone, which react with slightly acidic rainwater that drains into joints and fissures, dissolving some of the limestone. This process eventually forms caves and other features, and the water sometimes surfaces as springs many miles away. I thought, "That's amazingly simple."

Even though I have noticed many sinkholes and have been in numerous caves, I never would have imagined this amazing world of karst beneath our feet. Some hikes through karst territory include Edwin Warner Park Geology Trail (hike 3), two hikes in Cedars of Lebanon State Park (hikes 14 and, 16), and two hikes in Barfield Crescent Park in Murfreesboro (hikes 23 and 24).

Murfreesboro Greenway: Manson Pike Trail

This paved trail leads to an impressive pedestrian bridge, about 900 feet long, over the West Fork of the Stones River. The walk along Lytle Creek is both scenic and relaxing. Much of the trail is in the woods and affords good opportunities to hear and see birds. This linear trail in Murfreesboro is part of the city's greenway system.

Start: Manson Pike Trail trailhead adjacent to the small parking area
Distance: 2 miles out and back
Approximate hiking time: 1 hour
Difficulty: Easy due to wide paved trail
Trail surface: Asphalt
Best season: Year-round
Other trail users: Joggers, inline skaters, bicyclists, wheelchairs, strollers, dog walkers
Canine compatibility: Leashed dogs permitted
Fees and permits: None required
Schedule: Dawn to one hour before dusk

Maps: USGS: Murfreesboro; large trail maps board near each trailhead
Trail contact: Murfreesboro Greenway System, 697 Barfield Crescent Road., Murfreesboro, TN 37128; (615) 890-5333; www .murfreesborotn.gov
Other: Restrooms and water fountains are available at the trailhead. There is no potable water or restrooms on the trail. Take adequate water, use insect repellant and sunscreen, and wear a hat.

Finding the trailhead: From the east side of Nashville, take I-40 East via the ramp on the left toward Knoxville and go 4 miles. Keep right to take I-40 East, exit 213A, toward Chattanooga and go 24.5 miles. Take Manson Pike, exit 76, and go 0.2 mile. Take the Medical Center Parkway ramp and go 0.1 mile, then take a slight left onto Manson Pike and go 0.1 mile. Stay straight to get onto the Medical Center Parkway and follow the parkway for 2.8 miles. Turn left onto Searcy Street and go 0.1 mile to 1208 Searcy St. on the right. Proceed on the park road to the parking area and trailhead. *DeLorme Tennessee Atlas & Gazetteer:* Page 38, A2. GPS: N35 51.44' / W86 24.76'

26

Murfreesboro has realized the hiking possibilities within its city limits. First they considered the available scenery and topography. The free-flowing Stones River is the crown jewel, and the creeks that feed it shine brightly as well. The open space created by the preserved Stones River Battlefield already had trails, so it was a matter of connecting city greenways to this existing system. Like other cities, Murfreesboro strung their greenways along the Stones and its tributaries, eliminating unnecessary and costly acquisition of private property. Furthermore, these streamside floodplains have limited uses, so what better than a trail that can be used for exercising, commuting, and simply an excuse for being in the out-of-doors?

The Manson Pike Trail, a 1-mile track, heads south, reaching the Stones River, and then southeast, paralleling Lytle Creek, on the outbound leg, reversing the directions on the inbound leg. Start at the Manson Pike Trail trailhead adjacent to the small paved parking area. There is a kiosk with a large trail map and a boat ramp that leads down to the Stones River, along with two metal benches, a water fountain, and restroom. The trailhead serves as a connector north to the Redoubt

A family of hikers rests on a large slab of limestone next to the small waterfalls on Stones River on the Mason Pike Trail.

Brannon Trailhead and south to Overall Street Trailhead (the turnaround point of this hike) and the Old Fort Park Trailhead.

Turn right onto the trail, with the river on the left. Go under the Manson Pike overpass and immediately reach a path on the left that leads to a large flat slab of limestone along the river's edge. Waders, fishermen, and dog walkers will be spread out across the limestone. Rapids and small waterfalls form this part of the river. This is a very scenic view and deserves a little time to appreciate it and possibly take a few photos. Return to the trail and turn left, heading south.

Watch for a huckleberry tree on the right. In the spring and early summer, it bears fruit that resembles a blackberry and is edible. Birds and squirrels treat the fruit as ambrosia and fight to get to it. Sometimes overripe fruit will ferment while on the tree. This can lead to an amazing situation—tipsy birds and squirrels performing wild antics, sometimes even falling from the tree. Try not to step on the fruit, as it leaves a purple stain.

Reach a pedestrian bridge over the Stones River. The bridge is 900 feet long and has an observation deck near the middle. There is a color-coded map and a Y at the observation deck. Take the right branch, which is color-coded green and leads to the Overall Street Trailhead. The left branch leads to the Fortress Rosecrans Trailhead. At the end of the bridge, follow the trail as it heads into the woods. This pleasant area seems almost parklike.

The trail heads generally southeast as it reaches Lytle Creek. An access path on the right leads to the creek. Pass a large block of limestone on the right that is covered with moss and lichens. The trail weaves right, left, and right but still heads generally southeast. Listen for the bubbly sound of small rapids in the creek, whose water level can vary greatly depending on the amount of rainfall. Some limestone outcrops near the water's edge can be used as benches. The branches of hardwood trees form an arch over the creek, making this is the prettiest and most restful spot on the hike. Return to the trail and turn right.

Pass a shaded bench on the right near the creek. Reach a bike parking area that has a bench, a trail map board, and information signs about the defense of Fortress Rosecrans. In a very short distance, reach the turnoff for the Overall Street Trailhead. Proceed to the Overall Street Trailhead. This is a good spot to stop and backtrack to the trailhead.

🌿 **Green Tip:**
Don't take souvenirs home with you. This means natural materials such as plants, rocks, shells, and driftwood as well as historic artifacts such as fossils and arrowheads.

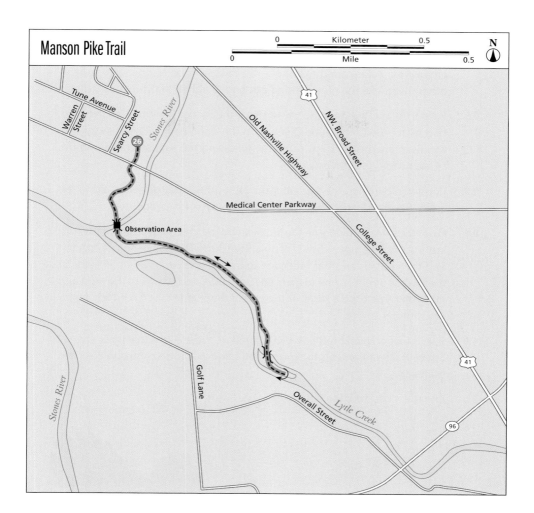

MILES AND DIRECTIONS

0.0 Start at the Manson Pike Trail trailhead adjacent to the small parking area. Head south and then bear east to the river.

0.1 After following the trail for less than 30 feet toward the West Fork of the Stones River, turn right at the river and a boat launch area and then follow along the river and under the Manson Pike overpass. Immediately reach a path connecting to the trail on the left. The river is on the left and to the east. Take a short out and back to see the falls and explore the river's edge. Return to the asphalt trail and turn left, heading generally southwest.

0.3 Cross a long (about 900 feet) pedestrian bridge. There is an observation area with a color-coded map near the center of the bridge, with exits to other trails. Take the green-coded exit on the right toward Overall Street.

0.5 Follow the trail as it bears left, away from the Stones River, toward the junction with Lytle Creek. Lytle Creek is on the right, about 30 feet away, and comes in and out of view. Continue following the asphalt trail along the creek, heading southeast.

0.7 Continue following the asphalt trail in a southeasterly direction along the creek. Several clearings allow access to the creek for exploration.

0.9 Pass limestone boulders on the left. Reach a bench, a map board of the trail, and information signs about Fortress Rosecrans. The trail bends slightly left and then passes another trail coming in from the right. This trail leads to the Overall Street Trailhead and Old Fort Park. Take the trail to the right and immediately cross a bridge. At the end of the bridge take a hard left, heading south.

1.0 Reach a wood picnic table on the left and a concrete area that is the Overall Street Trailhead, then turn around and backtrack to the Manson Pike Trail trailhead.

2.0 End the hike at the trailhead.

The mockingbird is the state bird of Tennessee.
It can mimic over forty different sounds.

Murfreesboro Greenway: College Street Pond Loop

This is a great hike for folks who enjoy ponds and the creative use of a landfill, as well as sun lovers. The loop leads to a pond with a small island containing formal gardens, a reception center, and a gazebo. Small waterfalls flow from the upper level to the lower level of the pond, which also includes three floating fountains. Birds thrive in this man-made habitat.

Start: Pond Loop Trail trailhead adjacent to the parking area off College Street
Distance: 1.7-mile clockwise loop
Approximate hiking time: 1 hour
Difficulty: Easy due to wide paved trail
Trail surface: Asphalt
Best season: September to June
Other trail users: Joggers, inline skaters, bicyclists, wheelchairs, strollers, dog walkers
Canine compatibility: Leashed dogs permitted
Fees and permits: None required
Schedule: Dawn to dusk

Maps: USGS Murfreesboro; large mounted trail map near each trailhead
Trail contact: Murfreesboro Greenway System, 697 Barfield Crescent Road, Murfreesboro, TN 37128; (615) 890-5333; www.murfreesborotn.gov
Other: There are restrooms at the reception center, but the center is not open every day. There is no potable water or restrooms on the trail, and little to no shade. Take adequate water, use insect repellant and sunscreen, and wear a hat.

Finding the trailhead: From the east side of Nashville, take I-40 East via the ramp on the left toward Knoxville and go 4 miles. Keep right to take I-24 East, exit 213A, toward Chattanooga and go 23.3 miles. Merge onto TN 840 East via exit 74B toward Lebanon and go 1.9 miles. Merge onto Northwest Broad Street, exit 55A, toward Murfreesboro and go 2.7 miles. Turn right onto Thompson Lane and go 0.3 mile, then turn left onto Old Nashville Highway and go 0.1 mile. Turn right onto West College Street and go 0.3 mile to 1902 West College St. in Murfreesboro. Proceed to the parking area and trailhead. *DeLorme Tennessee Atlas & Gazetteer:* Page 38, A2. GPS: N35 52.14' / W86 25.26'

THE HIKE

Talk about turning a lemon into lemonade! The city of Murfreesboro took an eyesore of an old landfill and turned it into Gateway Island, the centerpiece of a lake and trail system that connects to the greater Murfreesboro Greenway system. The site can be rented for weddings and other events. The trails are great for hikers and city residents who would otherwise have avoided the locale. Now it attracts wildlife to the water and repeat visitors who like to view the fountains and waterfalls while walking the well-designed and landscaped greenspace.

Formally known as the Gateway Trail, this 1.7-mile clockwise loop heads south, then southeast, then west, and finishes heading north. There is little to no tree can-

The author takes a time-out after hiking the new Gateway Trail at College Street.

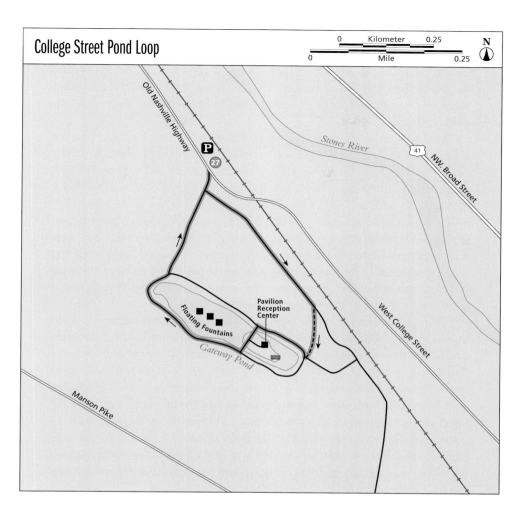

College Street Pond Loop

opy to furnish shade, so this hike is best done in the early morning or late afternoon. On a cold winter day, the open sunny track will feel great. Begin your hike at the Pond Loop trailhead, which has a kiosk with a large color-coded map and several benches. Use caution crossing College Street and make a hard left onto the paved trail. Go up a slight hill and bear right. Continue heading south until reaching a Y and take the left branch. Park lights mounted on tall metal posts alternately line the edge of the trail. Pass a bench on the left, constructed from steel rods. These benches are a signature feature of the trail. Most of the area around the trail is mowed grass.

Bear right and go slightly up, past a large meadow on the right that covers a closed landfill. Throughout this hike, visual control is maintained over the entire trail. Stop at a park bench on the left and look toward the pond and island. Three fountains can be seen in the pond, as well as some commercial buildings beyond the island. The water, grassy meadow area, and a few trees make this area good habitat for numerous species of birds, including killdeer, robin, dove, and red-wing blackbird.

Bear right, then left, as the trail heads slightly down. Reach a Y and take the right branch. Mature hardwood trees, including oak, are on the right. In a short distance reach a Y that has formal flower plantings around it and two benches with a large map board between them. Take the right branch and head a bit north and then west. Turn left and cross a bridge southwesterly onto the island, which contains a reception center, a gazebo, formal flower plantings, numerous benches, and several picnic tables. A stream crosses the island and forms two small waterfalls that tumble down into the pond. This is a pleasant area and a good spot to rest and snap a few photos. Cross over the bricked surface to the opposite side of the island and cross a steel bridge to pick up the trail. Turn right, heading northwest, with a grassy meadow on the left and the pond on the right.

Pass several benches on the right, facing the pond. This is the best location to view the three floating fountains in the center of the pond. Continue following the trail north toward a three-story commercial building. Notice the gushing water flowing from a pipe at the head of the pond. This is repurified water from the city's water and sewer department. A large flock of Canada geese and a few other water-birds frolic in the fresh water. Follow the trail around the pond to a Y and take the right branch, heading east for a short distance and then north. The left branch is a sidewalk that leads to a medical clinic. Continue following the trail along the large meadow (the closed landfill) on the right and pass a fenced area that contains a gas burner used to burn methane escaping from the landfill. Almost immediately reach a Y and take the left branch to backtrack to the trailhead.

MILES AND DIRECTIONS

0.0 Start at the Pond Loop Trail trailhead adjacent to the paved parking area off College Street.

0.1 Follow the asphalt trail and within 100 feet reach the stop sign at College Street. Cross College Street, using caution, and follow the trail, making a hard left and heading southeast.

0.5 Continue following the trail in a southeasterly direction. A trail comes in from the right; turn right onto this trail, heading west. There is a meadow to the right.

0.6 Reach a Y and take the right branch still heading west, at a lamppost on the left. Continue following the trail west.

0.7 Reach a Y and take the right branch, heading temporarily north, past the southeastern end of the pond, and then west. Pass a bench with formal flower plantings around it. A trail map board is between them. The island and pond are just ahead.

0.9 Follow the trail along the pond to the island, crossing one of two metal bridges. Cross the bridge on the west side of the island, reach a T with the main trail, and take the right branch, still heading west. Follow the trail, with the pond on the right, as it makes a hard right, heading north.

1.3 Reach a Y and take the right branch, heading northeast. (The left branch is a sidewalk leading to a medical clinic.) Follow the trail as it bends around the north end of the pond.

1.4 Reach a Y and take the left branch, heading north. (The right branch follows back along the pond.) A grassy meadow is on the right. Continue following the trail a short distance until reaching a Y. Take the left branch and backtrack to the trailhead.

1.7 End the hike at the trailhead.

Stones River National Battlefield: Cotton Field Trail & Boundary Trail

This is the hike for Civil War buffs. The trail goes through major action sites of the Battle of Murfreesboro, fought from December 31, 1862, to January 2, 1863. More than 80,000 troops participated in the battle. Interpretive signs and cannons from the war are placed near the trail. A side trail leads to the Slaughter Pen, where one of the bloodiest engagements of the battle was waged.

Start: Cotton Field Trail trailhead adjacent to the visitor center parking area
Distance: 3.1-mile clockwise loop, with a short out and back
Approximate hiking time: 2 hours
Difficulty: Easy due to flat trail
Trail surface: Paved roads, dirt
Best season: September to June
Other trail users: Joggers, dog walkers, bicyclists, slow-moving vehicles on one section
Canine compatibility: Leashed dogs permitted
Fees and permits: None required
Schedule: 8:00 a.m. to 6:00 p.m. in summer; 8:00 a.m. to 5:00 p.m. in winter
Maps: USGS: Walterhill; trail maps and brochures available at visitor center and online at www.nps .gov/stri
Trail contact: National Park Service, 3501 Old Nashville Hwy., Murfreesboro, TN 37129; (615) 893-9501; www.nps.gov/stri
Other: Water fountains and restrooms are available at the visitor center. There is no potable water or restrooms on the trail. Take adequate water, use insect repellant and sunscreen, and wear a hat.

Finding the trailhead: From the east side of Nashville, take I-40 East via the ramp on the left toward Knoxville and go 4 miles. Keep right to take I-24 East, exit 213A, toward Chattanooga and go 23.3 miles. Merge onto TN 840 East via exit 74B toward Lebanon and go 1.9 miles. Merge onto Northwest Broad Street, exit 55A, toward Murfreesboro and go 2.7 miles. Turn right onto Thompson Lane and go 0.3 mile; turn left onto Old Nashville Highway and go 0.1 mile (you're circling around to head northwest). Turn left onto West College Street and go 0.1 mile; West College Street becomes Old Nashville Highway. Go 0.7 mile to enter the National Park Service area. Follow the park road to the parking area and visitor center. *DeLorme Tennessee Atlas & Gazetteer:* Page 38, A1. GPS: N35 52.86' / W86 26.09'

THE HIKE

Before your hike, stop at the National Park Service visitor center to pick up a trail map and brochures. The visitor center also shows a short, interesting movie featuring highlights of the Battle of Murfreesboro, which was fought from December 31, 1862, to January 2, 1863. Watching the movie can add an extra dimension to the hike. This was a major battle, involving a combined total of more than 80,000 troops commanded by Union general William Starke Rosecrans and Confederate general Braxton Bragg. The battle waged back and forth with the outcome uncertain, until Union troops were able to stop the Confederates short of the Nashville Pike and Nashville-Chattanooga Railroad, and General Bragg retreated toward Chattanooga. There were 13,000 casualties during the three-day battle.

This 3.1-mile clockwise loop heads south, then west, and finishes heading north. Short sections of the hike border the park's tour road, while others are in the woods. Start at the Cotton Field Trail trailhead located at the west side of the visitor center parking area and head west. Two cannons can be seen across the tour road on the right. Mowed grass and cedar trees are near the trail's edge, and Old Nashville Highway is visible about 600 feet to the north.

Cannons lie abandoned near the Slaughterhouse, where Union general Philip Sheridan held off the attacking Confederate troops during the Civil War.

Reach an information sign that tells how 30,000 Union soldiers, supported by a large number of cannons, held back the Confederate charge across the cotton field. Bear right from the sign and pass a few slabs of limestone. Continue straight ahead until reaching three cannons on the left. Do a short out and back to investigate the area to view the cannons, which were actually used in the war. Parson's Artillery held this position. After returning to the trail, continue until reaching a T; take the right branch, heading south on the Old McFadden Road. Follow the trail as it leads slightly up and through heavy woods, providing welcome shade.

Come to a Y and take the right branch, still heading generally south although the trail weaves back and forth. A split-rail fence bordering woods is on the right side, and open fields are on the left. Bear hard left, heading west, and reach a Y near the park's tour road. Take the left branch and walk along the edge of the road for a short distance. Use caution because there will be slow-moving vehicles on the road. Pass Tour Stop 2, and at the back of the small parking area, take the trail south to the Slaughter Pen, where Union general Phil Sheridan's two-hour stand in the cedar thickets saved the day by holding back the charging Confederates. There are several information signs and pieces of abandoned artillery here. Reach a split-rail fence and backtrack to the trail, which is now the Boundary Trail, and head west.

Fragile cedar glades are located near the trail. These are home to the purple coneflower and Pyne's ground plum, both endangered plant species. Access into the glades is prohibited. Continue heading generally west in the woods. The trail goes over some uneven rocky terrain, so use caution. Bear hard right, heading north. Poison ivy grows near the trail's edge and into the woods, so learn to recognize this three-leaved hike spoiler. Watch for the white blazes identifying the Boundary Trail while continuing north.

Reach a cross-section and take the left branch, heading northwest, for a short distance. Pass some trenches on the right, about 10 feet from the trail. These shallow trenches were dug by soldiers to protect themselves from enemy gunfire. Continue north and slightly northeast and pass some earthworks, which are simply dirt, logs, and stones piled up to protect the soldiers. Bear right, heading past limestone slabs and outcrops on both the right and left. Reach a Y and take the left branch that leads to a small picnic area adjacent to the visitor center parking area, ending your hike.

> *During the Battle of Murfreesboro, a touching moment occurred on New Year's Eve when the armies were camped near each other and both bands joined in playing "Home Sweet Home."*

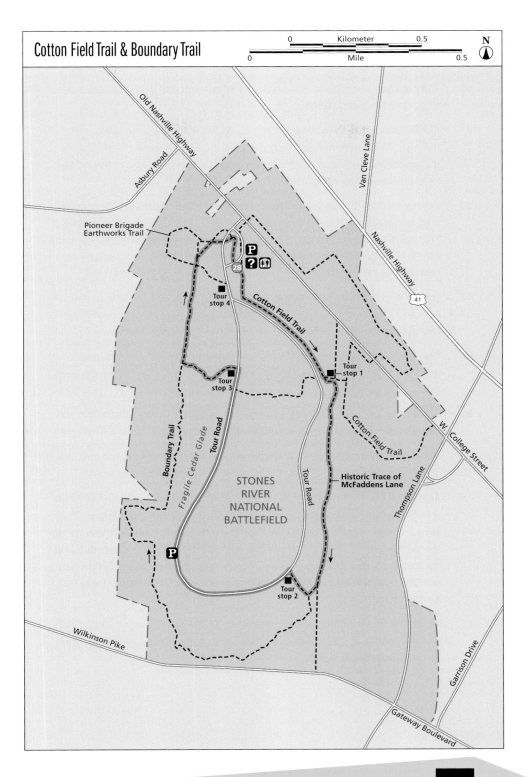

Cotton Field Trail & Boundary Trail

0 Kilometer 0.5
0   Mile   0.5

N

Old Nashville Highway

Asbury Road

Van Cleve Lane

Nashville Highway

Pioneer Brigade
Earthworks Trail

P
?

28

Tour
stop 4

Cotton Field Trail

41

Tour
stop 3

Tour
stop 1

Boundary Trail

Fragile Cedar Glade

Tour Road

Cotton Field Trail

STONES
RIVER
NATIONAL
BATTLEFIELD

Tour Road

Historic Trace of
McFaddens Lane

W. College Street

Thompson Lane

P

Tour
stop 2

Garrison Drive

Wilkinson Pike

Gateway Boulevard

0.0 Start at the Cotton Field Trail trailhead adjacent to the parking area at the visitor center and head west.

0.1 Almost immediately pass two Civil War cannons across the park road on the right. (Use caution if crossing the park road to examine them.) The visitor center will be directly to the left. Follow the asphalt trail as it heads hard left, temporarily heading east.

0.3 Pass three caissons on the left, across the park road. Continue following the trail, generally southeast, and pass an information sign. The Old Nashville Pike can be seen to the left. Bear right from the information sign. The cotton field where a major battle took place is on the left, and the park tour road and fields are on the right. Continue heading south on the trail.

0.5 Follow the trail hard left, temporarily heading east, and then bear right. A wood fence is to the right. Pass an information sign for Parson's Artillery. A mowed area leads to three cannons on the left about 30 feet away.

0.6 Reach a T and take the right branch, still heading south. Continue following the trail south, which is the Old McFadden Road. A wood fence parallels the trail on the right.

0.7 Reach a Y and take the right branch, still heading south. Follow the trail straight as it leads between woods on the right and left.

1.0 Take a hard left where a 5-foot-high split-rail fence intersects the trail. Follow the fence, which is on the right, as it leads toward the tour road.

1.2 Reach the Y with the tour road. Turn left on the road and walk on the grass along its edge. Tour traffic on the road is very slow, but use caution. Tour Stop 2, with a small parking area, is on the left. Take the trail at the back of the parking area, heading south through the woods, for a short out and back to the Slaughter Pen. Pass an information sign describing Union general Sheridan's stand and a sign about abandoned cannons on the trail. Backtrack to the tour road.

1.5 Reach the tour road and turn left, walking on the grass along the road. Follow the road as it bears right, heading west. Make a hard right, following the road as it heads north.

2.0 Continue on the grass along the road and pass a sign indicating a fragile cedar glade on the right. Do not enter this area. Within 0.1 mile pass another fragile cedar glade area. Continue following the tour road north.

2.4 Pass Tour Stop 3. This is near the cotton field, which is to the right. Go to the back of the Tour Stop 3 parking area and take the connector trail to the Boundary Trail. Head a short distance west and then north into the woods. Pass an information sign about the fight for the cedars. Follow the mulch Boundary Trail bearing right, heading temporarily west but still continuing generally north.

2.7 Reach a T and turn right, continuing on the Boundary Trail, which is now gravel surfaced. Pass the Pioneer Brigade trenches and turn hard left, going west for a short distance.

3.0 Bear right, heading north past the Pioneer Brigade earthworks. Make a hard right, heading east, and continue a short distance to a Y. Take the left branch, heading northeast. Continue following the trail through the woods to an opening.

3.1 End the hike at some picnic tables at the edge of the parking area, near the trailhead.

Stones River Greenway: Fortress Rosecrans Trail

Civil War aficionados will enjoy the short interpretive trail and boardwalk that explain the defense of Fortress Rosecrans. Defensive mounds still exist, and information signs tell where cannon sites and other features of the fort were. The trail crosses a long wooden bridge over the Stones River that has an observation area in the middle.

Start: Fortress Rosecrans Trail trailhead adjacent to the parking area
Distance: 2.3-mile counterclockwise loop
Approximate hiking time: 1.5 hours
Difficulty: Easy due to flat paved trail
Trail surface: Asphalt
Best season: Year-round
Other trail users: Joggers, inline skaters, bicyclists, wheelchairs, strollers, dog walkers
Canine compatibility: Leashed dogs permitted
Fees and permits: None required

Schedule: Daylight to a half hour before dark
Maps: USGS: Murfreesboro; large mounted trail map near each trailhead and on bridge
Trail contacts: National Park Service, 3501 Old Nashville Hwy., Murfreesboro, TN 37129; (615) 893-9501; www.nps.gov/stri. Murfreesboro Greenway System, 697 Barfield Crescent Road, Murfreesboro, TN 37128; (615) 890-5333; www.murfreesborotn.gov.
Other: There is no potable water or restrooms on the trail.

Finding the trailhead: From the east side of Nashville, take I-40 East via the ramp on the left toward Knoxville and go 4 miles. Keep right to take I-24 East, exit 213A, toward Chattanooga and go 26.7 miles. Merge onto Old Fort Parkway, exit 78B, toward Murfreesboro and go 1.8 miles. Turn left onto Golf Lane and go 0.2 mile. Turn right to stay on Golf Lane and go 0.4 mile to 1024 Golf Lane, Murfreesboro, and the parking area adjoining the trailhead. *DeLorme Tennessee Atlas & Gazetteer:* Page 38, A2. GPS: N35 51.01' / W86 24.42'

THE HIKE

Union forces occupied Murfreesboro after the Battle of Murfreesboro, where Union general William Starke Rosecrans defeated Confederate general Braxton Bragg. The nearest Union supply depot was many miles away in Kentucky. General Rosecrans ordered the building of a fort to serve as a supply depot for the 40,000 soldiers in the area. This became the largest enclosed earthen fortification built during the Civil War. By the end of 1863, the fort was defended by more than fifty cannons. The Fortress Rosecrans area is administered by the National Park Service.

This 2.3-mile hike consists of a counterclockwise loop with a short out and back at the north end. The trail borders sections of the Stones River and Lytle Creek. Much of the area around the trail consists of mowed greenways and woods. Start at the Fortress Rosecrans Trail trailhead at the kiosk, which has a map board and several benches near it. Head south, leaving the Fortress Rosecrans Trail, down a slope toward Lytle Creek, about 200 feet away. Immediately cross a bridge over the creek and turn left, heading northwest. This is an interesting section of the trail, with woods, including cedar and mixed hardwoods, and a sprinkling of limestone rocks.

Even butterflies seem interested in Civil War history at the Fortress Rosecrans Trail.

Bear right, heading generally northwest, and reach a bench and two interpretive signs about the defense of Fortress Rosecrans. This section of the trail is heavily used by joggers, bicyclists, and folks pushing strollers. The woods change to mostly hardwoods, including oak, maple, and hickory. Pass two benches near the creek's edge and more limestone boulders. Mallard ducks can often be seen frolicking in the creek's riffles. Bear left, right, and left, still heading northwest.

Bear left, heading west, and reach a long wooden bridge, about 12 feet wide, over the Stones River. The bridge slopes up and then flattens to a large observation area in the middle. At the Y on the observation area, take the right branch, continuing north on the bridge as it slopes down. Continue north for about 0.3 mile to a path on the right that leads to a large flat limestone slab along the river's edge. There is a small waterfall and rapids here, and it's a very picturesque spot. Investigate the river—and the anglers, waders, and dog walkers attracted to it— and return to the trail. In a short distance reach the Manson Pike Trail trailhead and backtrack to the bridge.

At the Y at the observation area on the bridge, take the right branch, heading south by southwest, toward Fortress Rosecrans. The trail is bordered on the left by scattered trees and on the right by a two-rail fence. Continue south and slightly west, coming into the fort area. Mounds from Fortress Rosecrans earthworks are on the right and left, and the Old Fort Golf Course can be seen to the left. The wood fence continues to border the trail on the left. Reach a T that has a bench at its head, and take the left branch toward the main fort grounds. The right branch leads to playgrounds and the golf course. There is little to no shade in this area. Take a hard right, heading west, toward the Fortress Rosecrans boardwalk.

Come to a Y and take the left branch, heading northwest. Bicycles and skaters are not allowed on this section of the trail, which is administered by the National Park Service. The trail weaves a bit as it bears right and left. A few cedar and hardwood trees dot the area, which is filled with mounds. Reach the long boardwalk, the highlight of this portion of the hike. The boardwalk allows a better view of the fort grounds and numerous mounds. The mounds, called lunettes, were used as artillery platforms. Numerous information signs are mounted on the boardwalk. Spend some time enjoying the view and studying the signs.

After leaving the boardwalk, follow the trail as it tracks a weaving path, generally heading southeast. Reach a Y and take the left branch, passing several interpretive signs. One of the more interesting ones is titled "Toil and Mud" and describes

---

🌿 Green Tip:
Be green and stylish too—wear clothing made of
organic cotton and other recycled products.

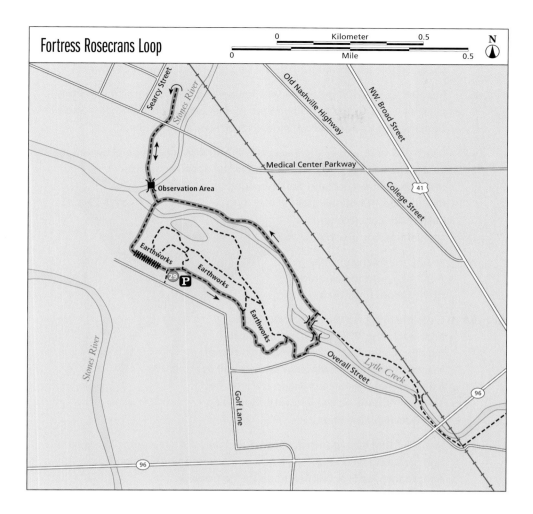

Fortress Rosecrans Loop

how soldiers worked around the clock to build the fort, which was surrounded by 1,400 feet of earthen walls. Mounds and scattered trees border the trail. Reach a Y and take the left branch. In a short distance reach a T with Golf Road and turn left to follow the sidewalk back to the trailhead.

MILES AND DIRECTIONS

0.0 Start at the Fortress Rosecrans Trail trailhead at the edge of the parking area and head south toward Lytle Creek.

0.1 Pass earthen mounds on the left. Lytle Creek is on the right, down a slope, about 200 feet away. Cross a bridge and turn left at the end. Follow the asphalt trail, continuing in a northerly direction.

0.2 Pass two benches on the left, along the creek's edge. Go down to the creek to investigate and then return to the trail, still heading generally north.

0.4 Bear left and then right as the trail squiggles a little. The trail follows the river, which is on the left side, about 25 feet away, and then bears away from the creek. A long wood bridge can be seen straight ahead.

0.5 Reach the bridge over the Stones River and cross the large observation area in the middle. At the Y at the end of the observation area, take the right branch and finish crossing the bridge. Continue following the concrete and asphalt trail northeast.

0.7 Reach the Manson Pike Trail trailhead and backtrack to the Stones River bridge.

0.9 Cross the bridge to the observation area and reach the Y. Take the right branch, heading generally south between two sets of fences. Continue following the asphalt trail as it approaches the Fortress Rosecrans area. Pass earthen mounds on the left, with the Old Fort Golf Course on the right.

1.1 Reach a T that has a bench at its head, and take the left branch. Take a hard right, heading west as the trail surface changes to brown aggregate. The right branch leads to ball fields and the golf course.

1.2 Reach a Y and take the left branch onto the Fortress Rosecrans Trail. Almost immediately reach a boardwalk that overlooks the earthen mounds of the fort. Take time to read the information signs on the boardwalk that describe the defensive nature of the fort. Follow around the boardwalk and down to the asphalt trail, and follow it straight east.

1.5 Continue following the trail generally east. Pass some mounds that reach to the edge of the trail and an interpretive sign labeled "Toil and Mud." Reach a Y and take the left branch, then almost immediately reach a T and take the right branch, still heading generally east.

1.7 Pass a path on the right that leads to a Civil War cannon. Reach a Y and take the left branch, heading toward the road and parking area. Just ahead of the road, turn left onto the sidewalk and follow it to the trailhead.

2.3 End the hike at the trailhead.

Murfreesboro Greenway: Thompson Lane to Broad Street

This hike is for those interested in learning more about the Battle of Murfreesboro. A short out and back on a historic lane takes you to McFadden Farm, where Confederate General Breckinridge's troops nearly overwhelmed the Union forces. This is followed by a walk along the West Fork of the Stones River, with a stop at the observation platform along the river's edge.

Start: Historic Lane to McFadden Farm Trail trailhead at the northeast side of the parking area
Distance: 2.6 miles out and back. (0.4 mile for the McFadden Farm segment and 2.2 miles for Thompson Lane to Broad Street)
Approximate hiking time: 1.5 hours
Difficulty: Easy due to flat paved trail
Trail surface: Asphalt, gravel
Best season: September to June
Other trail users: Joggers, inline skaters, bicyclists, wheelchairs, strollers, dog walkers
Canine compatibility: Leashed dogs permitted

Fees and permits: None required
Schedule: Dawn to dusk
Maps: USGS: Walterhill; large mounted trail map at trailhead
Trail contact: Murfreesboro Greenway System, 697 Barfield Crescent Road, Murfreesboro, TN 37128; (615) 890-5333; www.murfreesborotn.gov
Other: A shelter at the trailhead has water and restrooms. There is no potable water or restrooms on the trail. Take adequate water, use insect repellant and sunscreen, and wear a hat. Bikes are not allowed on McFadden Lane.

Finding the trailhead: From the east side of Nashville, take I-40 East via the ramp on the left toward Knoxville and go 4 miles. Keep right to take I-24 East, exit 213A, toward Chattanooga and go 23.3 miles. Merge onto TN 840 East via exit 74B toward Lebanon and go 1.9 miles. Merge onto Northwest Broad Street via exit 55A toward Murfreesboro and go 2.7 miles. Turn left onto North Thompson Lane and go 0.6 mile to 2240 North Thompson Lane, Murfreesboro, and the parking area and trailhead. *DeLorme Tennessee Atlas & Gazetteer:* Page 38, A2. GPS: N35 53.20' / W86 25.38'

THE HIKE

Murfreesboro has created a boon for hikers by connecting trails and routing them along river and creek floodplains that normally would be considered unusable. The city has built bridges over the Stones River that connect trails, and it has incorporated the Stones River National Battlefield, site of the Battle of Murfreesboro, a major Civil War battle, and the Cotton Field Trail into its greenway trail system. This type of planning and creativity may be the model for in-city hiking.

The Thompson Lane to Broad Street Trail is one of ten trails in the extensive Murfreesboro Greenway system and forms the northern terminus of the system. Stay on the right side of this 12-foot-wide multiuse paved trail to give other users the opportunity to pass, and always give notice when passing people (on the left) using strollers or wheelchairs.

This "double" hike begins with a short (0.4 mile) out and back on the McFadden Farm Trail that heads north, then west, and backtracks to the trailhead. After returning to the trailhead, you then go to the right to the Thompson Lane to Broad

The West Fork of Stones River runs parallel to the historic Thompson Lane to Broad Street Trail.

Thompson Lane to Broad Street

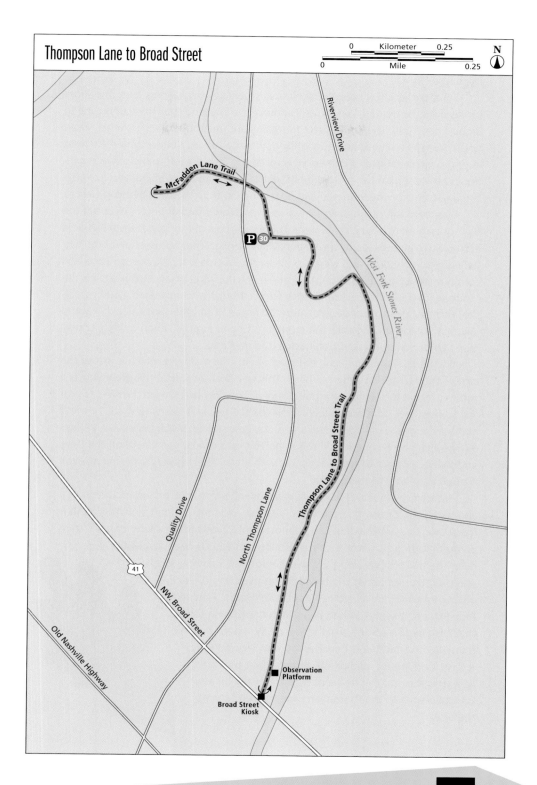

Street trailhead. This 2.2-mile out and back heads east, then south, and backtracks from Broad Street.

Start at the kiosk near the shelter, adjacent to the parking area. The kiosk serves both the Historic Lane to McFadden Farm Trail and the Thompson Lane to Broad Street Trail. There are water fountains and restrooms in the shelter. Head north from the trailhead and go slightly downhill and past a picnic table. Bear right after the picnic table and immediately reach a Y. Take the left branch, which continues on McFadden Lane. The right branch is a dead end. The trail passes a canoe-launching area on the Stones Rivers. Bear left away from the river, heading west.

Bear hard left, still heading west, and reach an informational sign about the McFadden Farm Artillery Monument. This area is part of the Stones River National Battlefield, administered by the National Park Service. The main section of the battlefield is to the south and west. Go under the overpass for Thompson Lane and continue west. Head up a slight slope and reach the ridge where Union artillery fire repulsed Confederate General Breckinridge's, troops who sustained 1,800 casualties. This was the final engagement in the Battle of Murfreesboro. Reach a Y and take the right branch toward the monument honoring the Union artillery teams. Stop at the monument and backtrack to the trailhead.

Go to the Thompson Lane to Broad Street Trail trailhead, which is just to the east of the McFadden Lane trailhead. This trail and section of the greenway is a certified arboretum. Follow the trail downhill, heading east toward the West Fork of the Stones River. Continue following the asphalt trail as it bears right, still heading east, past a group of large limestone rocks. Pass several metal benches and then a large apartment complex on the right. The river can be seen through the trees on the left, along with residences across the river. There is very little shade, even though trees line the trail's edge.

After traveling about 0.75 mile, reach two benches and an informational sign about Harkers Crossing, a particularly heroic incident during the Battle of Murfreesboro. Pass a picnic table and almost immediately reach a wood observation platform jutting out over the river. Residences can be seen across the river. The trail follows along the river's edge, still heading south, and then crosses under the Broad Street overpass. A fence is on the right side and a path comes in from the left, leading to Broad Street. Take the path to Broad Street and reach a kiosk that has a large map board of the greenway system. A water fountain, bike rack, and benches are also located here. A large parking lot adjoins the Broad Street trailhead, and several stores can be seen. Stop and rest a bit and then backtrack to the Thompson Lane trailhead to end the hike.

McFadden Farm Segment

0.0   Start at the Historic Lane to McFadden Farm Trail adjacent to the parking area and head north.

0.1   Bear right and go down a slope. Within 100 feet reach a Y and take the left branch (the right branch dead-ends). Bear right and then hard left and pass an information sign. Follow the trail under the Thompson Lane over-pass, and pass the McFadden Farm sign. On the right is the Union Artillery Monument, on the ridge.

0.2   Reach a Y and take the right branch, heading temporarily north. The Union Artillery Monument is directly to the right. Stop and backtrack to the trail-head (continuing on will lead to the Stones River National Battlefield).

0.4   Reach the McFadden Farm Trail trailhead and go to the adjoining Thomp-son Lane to Broad Street trailhead.

Thompson Lane to Broad Street

0.0   Start at the Thompson Lane to Broad Street Trail trailhead, heading east for a short distance.

0.1   Follow the asphalt trail as it bears left, right, and left, generally heading southeast. Pass a park bench on the right; the West Fork of the Stones River is on the left. Pass a mowed clearing on the right.

0.3   Continue following the asphalt trail, heading generally south along the riv-er's edge. The river is about 30 feet away. Pass several metal park benches. An apartment complex is on the right.

0.6   The trail heads generally south as it passes an information sign about the devastation from the 2009 tornado. Continue following the trail south, with the river on the left.

0.75   Pass a concrete area with a bike stand and an information sign describing Harkers Crossing. A dirt path leads down to the river. Continue following the asphalt trail generally south.

1.0   Reach a wooden observation platform over the river. Residences can be seen across the river, which is about 125 feet wide. Return to the trail and continue heading south. Pass under the Broad Street overpass and con-tinue straight and slightly up.

1.1 Reach the kiosk at Broad Street, with a water fountain, bike rack, and large map board. This is the trailhead for the Broad Street to Thompson Lane Trail. A large parking area and 84 Lumber store are just past the kiosk. Stop at the kiosk, then turn around and backtrack to the Thompson Lane trailhead.

2.2 End the hike at the trailhead.

Rotting logs support mosses, lichens, and other parasites on the Thompson Lane to Broad Street Trail.

Bowie Woods: Bowie Lakes Loop

This hike is for lovers of small lakes, woods, birds, and wildlife. The trail passes fives lakes as it meanders up and down through mixed forests that include loblolly pine, oak, and hickory. Deer are frequently seen near the edge of the woods. Look for shorebirds near the edges of the lakes. See the amazing job the Bowie sisters did in reclaiming this land!

Start: At the parking area adjacent to the rest rooms
Distance: 4.6-mile counterclockwise loop
Approximate hiking time: 3 hours to allow time to explore lakes
Difficulty: Moderate due to length and some long inclines
Trail surface: Bark mulch, dirt
Best season: September to June
Other trail users: Dog walkers
Canine compatibility: Leashed dogs permitted
Fees and permits: None required
Schedule: 6:00 a.m. to 10:00 p.m. in summer; sunrise to 8:00 p.m. in winter
Maps: USGS: Craigfield; trail maps available at park office
Trail contact: Park Manager, Bowie Park, 7211 Bowie Lake Rd., Fairview, TN 37063; (615) 799-5544; www.fairview/tn.org
Other: Water fountains and rest-rooms are available at the park office and trailhead. There is no potable water or restrooms on the trail. Trails may be closed due to wet conditions; call ahead.

Finding the trailhead: From the west side of Nashville, take I-40 West and go 26.8 miles. Take TN 96, exit 182, toward Fairview and go 0.1 mile, then turn right onto TN 9 and go 4.7 miles. Merge onto TN 100 West and go 0.4 mile, then turn slight right onto Cox Pike. End at the entrance to Bowie Park in Fairview and follow the park road to the nature center parking area. *DeLorme Tennessee Atlas & Gazetteer:* Page 36, A3. GPS: N35 58.215' / W87 08.312'

THE HIKE

Several trails have been combined to allow this 4.6-mile counterclockwise loop to take in the best of Bowie Park's 722 acres. Stop at the park head-quarters/nature center to pick up a trail map and then drive a block to the picnic/playground/parking area and adjoining restrooms. There is a kiosk in front of the restroom building, with a large color-coded trail map. The Loblolly Loop Trail trailhead is down a short hill a very short distance west, toward Lake Van. Follow the Loblolly Loop Trail north, across the end of Lake Van. The lake is on the right, and Canada geese can often be seen scattered along the its edge. Cross a bridge and bear left at the end. In a short distance bear right, heading north, following the Loblolly Loop Trail. The terrain slopes gently up and down.

This corridor of pine trees on the Loblolly Loop Trail is unique and creates an air of solitude.

Bowie Lakes Loop

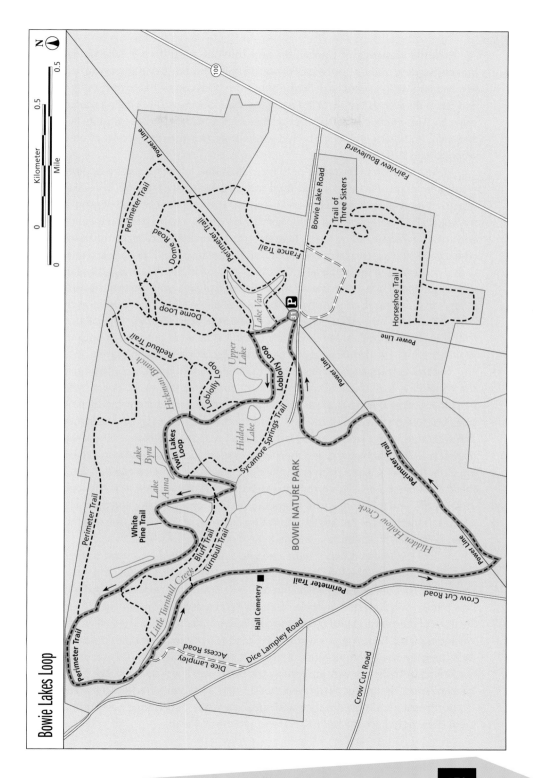

Pass the west side of Upper Lake and continue north to a Y. Take the left branch, heading slightly northeast. Follow the trail a short distance and take a hard left, heading west, toward Lake Byrd. Songs from birds can be heard as they fly in and out of the woods. Listen for the red-bellied woodpeckers' call, a rolling *churr* or *chiv-chiv*. This medium-size bird is easy to recognize, with its red head, white face and belly, and black-and-white-barred wings. Listen for the *rat-a-tat-tat* of other woodpeckers in the woods.

Make a hard left at the next Y onto Twin Lakes Trail, following southwest along the eastern edge of Lake Byrd. Lake Byrd and Lake Anna are called the Twin Lakes. Reach a three-way split in the trail and follow the extreme right branch, staying on the Twin Lakes Trail. Follow the trail a short distance until making a hard right at the edge of Lake Anna, heading north. Take a short path on the left to reach the beach, where you'll find a picnic table and kiosk. This is a great spot to kick back and relax, with a good view of the entire lake. Deer may be seen in this area, especially early in the morning or late in the afternoon. At the edge of the water, look for the water striders that appear to be walking on the surface of the lake. Little brushes at the base of their legs spread out, allowing them to do the walk-on-water thing. Return to the Twin Lakes Trail and immediately reach a Y; take the left branch onto the White Pine Trail. Head northwest and pass a small seasonal pond on the left.

The trail zigzags and reaches another Y; take the right branch, continuing on the White Pine Trail. The left branch is a short connector that drops down to the Bluff Trail. Follow down a slope and enter an interesting corridor created by pines trees bordering the edge of the trail. Hardwood trees, including oak, dogwood, and sycamore, form a woods on the left. Reach a T with the Perimeter Trail and take the left branch, heading west and then bearing south. Continue south until reaching Little Turnbull Creek, which is on the right. There are some pleasant rapids in the shallow creek. Bear slightly right to reach the edge of the creek, which is about 20 feet wide, and then ford it using stepping stones. Continue following the trail as it parallels the creek, watching for interesting outcrops of limestone. The trail then bears away from the creek, heading generally southeast.

Follow the trail as it bends right, heading south, and in a very short distance reach Hall Cemetery. This is a small cemetery from the Civil War, containing eleven tombstones of Confederate soldiers. Spend a little time at the cemetery, pondering how this spot was selected. Follow a steep, 40-degree slope downward for 150 feet. Sections of this trail are used by equestrians and mountain bikers. The trail weaves left and right but heads generally south. Proceed 0.7 mile south, at times bordering Dice Lampley Road, and then take a hard left, heading northeast. This section of the Perimeter Trail is not very interesting and has power lines overhead, but it can't be eliminated. The trail goes northeast for 0.5 mile and then turns hard left, heading northwest for a short distance, and crosses a heavy-duty bridge over Turnbull Creek. Bear right from the bridge and return to the trailhead.

0.0 Start at the Loblolly Loop Trail trailhead just north of the restrooms and adjacent to Lake Van, and head northwest.

0.1 Cross a bridge and bear left at the kiosk, heading northwest.

0.4 Bear right, passing a small unnamed pond. Bear left, heading southwest for a short distance, and then bear right, heading northwest.

0.6 Reach a Y and take the left branch, heading west on the Twin Lakes Loop. The right branch continues on the Loblolly Loop.

0.8 Follow the trail as it zigzags up and down small hills. Reach a Y and take the left branch, heading southwest on Twin Lakes Loop to Lake Bryd and Lake Anna.

1.0 Pass a bench and reach a three-way split in the trail. Continue straight on the rightmost leg, still on the Twin Lakes Loop. The middle leg leads to the Little Turnbull Trail, and the left leg leads to the Sycamore Springs Trail.

1.2 Follow the trail as it parallels Lake Anna. Take the path down to the lake, where there is a picnic table and a kiosk with a trail map. Return to the Twin Lakes Trail and at the Y near the kiosk, take the left branch onto the White Pine Trail, leading into the woods. Continue following the trail as it weaves through the trees, heading generally north.

1.9 Reach a Y and take the right branch, continuing on the White Pine Trail. The left branch drops down and connects to the Bluff Trail. Follow the White Pine Trail as it bears northwest. Pass a small unnamed lake on the right and reach a T. This is the junction with the Perimeter Trail. Take the left branch, heading west for a short distance, and then bear south.

2.3 Follow the trail as it bears right along Turnbull Creek, still heading generally south. Ford the 20-feet-wide shallow creek, using stepping stones. Follow the trail as it continues to zigzag southeast.

3.0 Bear right, heading south, and in a short distance pass Hall Cemetery on the right. Continue generally south for about 0.7 mile and then bear hard left, heading northeast, for a little more than 0.5 mile. Mountain bikers and equestrians use this section of the trail.

3.8   Bear hard left, heading northeast.

4.3   Make a hard left, heading northwest for a short distance, and then make a hard right, heading east toward the trailhead.

4.5   Cross a heavy-duty bridge and continue heading east toward the trailhead.

4.6   End the hike at the trailhead.

Thanks, Drs. Bowie

The dream and hard work of the three Bowie sisters reached fruition when they deeded what is now the 722-acre Bowie Park to the city of Fairview in 1989. Dr. Evangeline Bowie (1898–1992) and her sisters Bryd and Anna, also doctors, purchased the first 189 acres for $3,250 in 1954, against the wishes of their brothers. The land was barren, eroded, and full of ruts. Anna is said to have commented, "You could almost put a horse in some of them." It was estimated that thirty tons of topsoil were lost each year.

Undaunted, Evangeline led the way. She hired earth-moving equipment to build terraces, dig shallow lakes, and create a sustainable hydrology system. After talking to a state agriculture agent who advised the sisters that only loblolly pines could grow there, they took his advice and planted over 600,000 loblollies, which today serve to shelter some of the trails. Through the years these efforts showed progress in improving the worn-out land.

Some lakes failed or were not fed enough water to be sustainable, but Evangeline persevered, even going to the lakes when it was raining to analyze the water flow. State officials became interested in the work she was doing and sent several experts to analyze it. They were amazed! The hydrology system was so well designed and the soil had shown so much improvement that the state incorporated some of these ideas in other projects. Three of the five small lakes in the park are named for the sisters: Lake Van, Lake Byrd, and Lake Anna.

Bowie Park now serves the citizens of Fairfield and surrounding communities with 17 miles of hiking and equestrian trails. Most, with the exception of the Perimeter Trail, are very short and are named after a particular feature along the trail. They wind through several ecosystems, which include both lowland and bottomland wetlands, grasslands, pine forests, and oak/hickory forests.

The Bowie sisters were not wealthy, but through their frugality, hard work, and vision, hikers and non-hikers have a new destination. Thank you, Van, Bryd, and Anna.

Henry Horton State Park: Hickory Ridge Nature Loop

This is a great hike for geology and nature lovers. The self-guiding Nature Loop goes through karst terrain, with its abundance of limestone outcrops and sinkholes. Some of the sinkholes have short paths leading to them, allowing closer observation. The oak/hickory woods furnish habitat for deer and many species of birds.

Start: Hickory Ridge Nature Loop trailhead adjacent to the parking area

Distance: 2.4-mile lollipop

Approximate hiking time: 2 hours to allow time to read information signs

Difficulty: Moderate due to limestone outcrops

Trail surface: Dirt, limestone

Best season: Year-round

Other trail users: Dog walkers, joggers

Canine compatibility: Leashed dogs permitted

Fees and permits: None required

Schedule: 8:00 a.m. to 10:00 p.m. in summer; 8:00 a.m. to sundown in winter

Maps: USGS: Farmington; trail maps available at park office

Trail contact: Park Manager, Henry Horton State Park, 4209 Nashville Hwy., Chapel Hill, TN 37034; (931) 364-7724; www.state.tn.us/environment/parks

Other: Restrooms and water are available at the campground and park office. There is no potable water or restrooms on the trail, and mosquitoes and flies can be a nuisance, especially in the spring and fall. Take adequate water, use insect repellant and sunscreen, and wear a hat.

Finding the trailhead: From the south side of Nashville, take I-40 East via the ramp on the left toward Knoxville and go 0.9 mile. Merge onto I-65 South via exit 210 toward Huntsville and go 36.5 miles. Take US 412/TN 99, exit 46, toward Columbia and go 0.2 mile. Turn left onto US 412/Bear Creek Pike/TN 99 and continue to follow Bear Creek Pike/TN 99 for 4 miles. Turn slight right onto US 431 and go 0.8 mile, then turn right onto TN 99 and go 7.4 miles. Turn right onto US 31A and go 0.8 mile to 4209 Nashville Highway in Chapel Hill. Turn into the park entrance and follow the park road to the headquarters. *DeLorme Tennessee Atlas & Gazetteer:* Page 37, C6. GPS: N35 35.47' / W86 42.14'

The Hickory Ridge Nature Loop Trail is located in the 1,200-acre Henry Horton State Park near Chapel Hill. This 2.4-mile hike is a "balloon on a string," with the "string" heading northwest, north, south, and west until reaching the "balloon." Follow the balloon clockwise, generally heading west, north, and east, and backtrack on the string.

Stop at the park headquarters before your hike to pick up a map and the Hickory Ridge Nature Loop self-guiding brochure. In addition to numbered stops on the trail relating to the self-guiding brochure, several trees are identified by signs. Start at the trailhead adjacent to the parking area and immediately go into the woods, heading northwest. Low limestone outcrops border both sides of the trail.

A couple accompanies their dogs on the Hickory Ridge Trail.

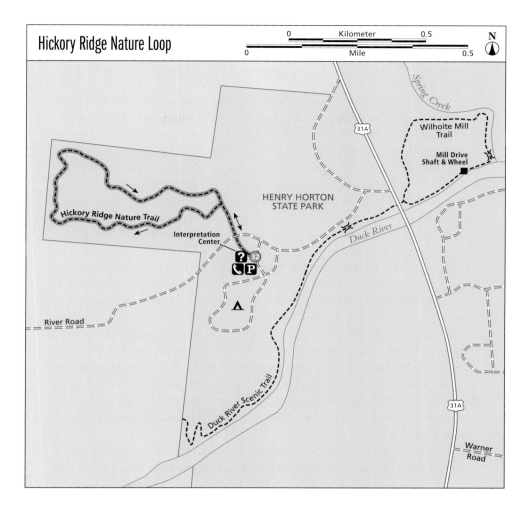

This area is a haven for birds, with the woods furnishing cover and the Duck River, a short distance to the east, furnishing water. Watch for the white-breasted nuthatch. It is smaller than a sparrow and sometimes called the "upside-down bird" due to its habit of climbing down tree trunks headfirst. It has a black cap, white face and breast, and bluish-colored wings. Its call is a low-pitched repeated *yank*. This is a fun bird for the family to observe.

Follow the trail until reaching and crossing the campground road. The trail continues on the other side of the road, leading back into the woods. Immediately reach a Y and take the left branch, heading south for a short distance and then west. Pass the campground, which is on the right. Ignore the many paths on the right leading to the campground as the trail weaves between the oak and hickory trees. Reach the Y at the start of the loop and take the left branch, heading west in a clockwise direction. Head slightly up into a very scenic section that includes wildflowers, woods, and limestone.

Continue following the trail as it bears south for about 0.2 mile and then turns hard left, heading east. This portion of the hike leads through typical karst terrain. A karst has little to no soil on the surface and is underlaid with limestone. Rain and other water seeping through the surface eventually erode the limestone, creating caves, sinkholes, and underground streams. Limestone outcrops and sinkholes are a karst's signature features. Reach a path on the left that leads to a large oblong sinkhole, about 20 feet away. Limestone lines its edge, and pieces of the collapsed "roof" can be seen along its sides. Those with a curious and somewhat adventurous nature may choose to climb around the hole and investigate more thoroughly—just be sure to use caution.

Return to the trail and bear left, then continue left in a semicircle as the trail follows around, generally heading east, and arrives at a mature oak/hickory forest. In the fall notice the hickory nuts on the ground. They are 1 to 1½ inches in diameter and are edible, but it is difficult to remove the husk and break open the shell. Crush some hickory leaves and note the faint apple smell. Move through the oak/hickory forest into a cedar forest. These are Eastern red cedars, and over time oak, hickory, and ash trees will grow taller than the cedars, shading them into oblivion. Post oak trees reach heights of 50 to 60 feet. This area contains numerous limestone outcrops and blocks, crevasses, and sinkholes. Sinkholes are scattered in the woods, and some reach the edge of the trail. The trail surface alternates between dirt and limestone.

Follow the yellow blazes and information signs, heading just slightly northeast. Ferns and mosses reach to the trail. Look for clumps of low-growing reindeer moss as it forms an undefined carpet. Deer graze on this moss and sometimes bed in it. Reindeer moss is a lichen, which is a special group that forms a community of algae living with fungi. Pass between groups of limestone outcrops, 2 to 4 feet high. Complete the loop by reaching the Y that started it, then backtrack and return to the trailhead.

MILES AND DIRECTIONS

0.0 Start at the Hickory Ridge Nature Loop trailhead about 100 yards north of the parking area. Follow the trail, which is marked with numbered information signs relating to the brochure, northwest. The trail is identified by yellow blazes.

0.2 Cross the asphalt park road, which leads to the campground. Use caution crossing the road. A marker identifies the trail on the opposite side of the road.

32

0.25   Pass an information sign about the scarlet oak on the right. The trail splits at the sign. Take the left branch and head south for a short distance, then make a hard right, heading west. This is the loop and it heads generally clockwise, with a lot of zigzagging. The park campground is on the right, hidden by trees.

0.3   Continue following the trail through the woods between limestone outcrops and sinkholes. A short path leads to a 12-foot-deep sinkhole that allows investigation. Use caution and return to the main trail. Bear slightly left and go over some limestone "steps."

0.5   Pass a sinkhole on the left, about 20 feet away, with a short path to it. Take the path to the oblong sinkhole, which is about 15 feet wide and 25 feet long. Return to the main trail and head left, almost immediately passing an information sign about sugar maples. Continue following the trail left in a small semicircle.

0.8   Stay on the trail by following the yellow blazes marked on the trees. Pass several information signs about trees located on the trail. Use caution around the many sinkholes and crevasses.

1.0   Reach an information sign about post oaks. Bear hard right at the sign and pass marker 8. The trail wanders left, right, and then left again through the oak/hickory woods and limestone outcrops.

1.2   Continue on the trail as it bobs slightly up and down. Pass the information sign about dogwoods. The trail flattens but continues to weave back and forth. Make a hard left and in 50 feet a hard right to reach marker 10. Bear right at the marker.

1.5   Pass several information signs and then reach the sign about Carolina buckthorns. Continue following the trail straight as the surface changes from dirt to limestone.

1.8   Low limestone outcrops are on the left. Pass a large, deep sinkhole on the right, about 12 feet off the trail.

1.9   Reach a path on the right that leads into the sinkhole mentioned at 1.8 miles. Do a short out and back to investigate the sinkhole and then return to the trail and head south.

2.1   Reach the Y where the loop started and take the right branch. Backtrack southeast to the trailhead.

2.4   End the hike at the trailhead.

Animal Tracks

Observing and attempting to identify animal tracks can add an extra dimension to a hike. Tracks are usually more prevalent near creeks and ponds, where the animals go for water. The most common mammal tracks to look for on the trails near Nashville are white-tailed deer, domestic dog, raccoon, squirrel, and opossum. Except for the squirrel and dog, seeing their tracks may be as close as you get to these animals.

The distinctive white-tailed deer track is among the easiest to find. Their prints are usually clear and large, 2 to 4 inches in length. The heart-shaped track is pointed and about 2 inches wide. If the trail passes through woods with trees bearing nuts, look for squirrel ramblings. Their front footprint shows four toes with sharp claws, while the rear print has five toes. If the squirrel was running or jumping, the rear prints are ahead of the front ones.

Henry Horton State Park: Wilhoite Mill Loop and Fisherman Trail

Those who enjoy history, woods, and rivers will especially like this hike. Explore the remains of the Wilhoite Mill, including a driveshaft attached to a large wheel, before continuing along the Duck River into the woods. Short, narrow paths lead to the river's edge, where you'll likely find a fisherman or two.

Start: Wilhoite Mill Trail trailhead adjacent to the south end of the parking area

Distance: 1.9-mile lollipop (1-mile loop with 0.9-mile out and back)

Approximate hiking time: 1.5 hours

Difficulty: Easy due to flat shaded trail

Trail surface: Dirt

Best season: Year-round

Other trail users: Dog walkers, joggers

Canine compatibility: Leashed dogs permitted

Fees and permits: None required

Schedule: 8:00 a.m. to 10:00 p.m. in summer; 8:00 a.m. to sundown in winter

Maps: USGS: Farmington; trail maps available at park office

Trail contact: Park Manager, Henry Horton State Park, 4209 Nashville Hwy., Chapel Hill, TN 37034; (931) 364-7724; www.state.tn.us/environment/parks

Other: Restrooms and water are available at the campground and park office. There is no potable water or restrooms on the trail. Take adequate water, use insect repellant and sunscreen, and wear a hat.

Finding the trailhead: From the south side of Nashville, take I-40 East via the ramp on the left toward Knoxville and go 0.9 mile. Merge onto I-65 South via exit 210 toward Huntsville and go 36.5 miles. Take US 412/TN 99, exit 46, toward Columbia and go 0.2 mile. Turn left onto US 412/Bear Creek Pike/TN 99 and continue to follow Bear Creek Pike/TN 99 for 4 miles. Turn slight right onto US 431 and go 0.8 mile, then turn right onto TN 99 and go 7.4 miles. Turn right onto US 31A and go 0.8 mile to 4209 Nashville Highway in Chapel Hill. Turn into the park entrance and follow the park road to the headquarters. *DeLorme Tennessee Atlas & Gazetteer:* Page 37, C6. GPS: N35 35.60' / W86 41.77'

THE HIKE

he Hickory Ridge Nature Loop Trail is located in the 1,200-acre Henry Horton
State Park near Chapel Hill. This 1.9-mile hike is a "balloon on a string," with
the "string" heading northeast until reaching the counterclockwise "balloon,"
which generally heads northeast, north, west, and south. This hike combines the
Wilhoite Mill Trail and a portion of the under-construction Duck River Scenic Trail,
which I call the Fisherman Trail. The Wilhoite Mill Trail is on the north side of the
Duck River, with sections paralleling the river and Spring Creek. It passes through
the site known as Wilhoite Mill, a once-thriving community that was active in the
late1800s. A mill operated by members of the Henry Horton family, which was
related to the founding Wilhoite family, was operational until 1959. The state purchased the site in 1959 to establish a park.

Before your hike, stop at the park headquarters to pick up a map. Start at the
trailhead adjacent to the gravel parking area and head northeast. Go down a slope
toward the Duck River and immediately reach some remnants of the old mill, which
have been left pretty much as they were found. A section of driveshaft attached to
a large wheel, which was probably used to turn the shaft, presents a good photo
opportunity. Bear left and pass a sign that points to the campground. The Duck

A number of mills were located along the Duck River in the 1800s. These remains are from a dam and
a mill.

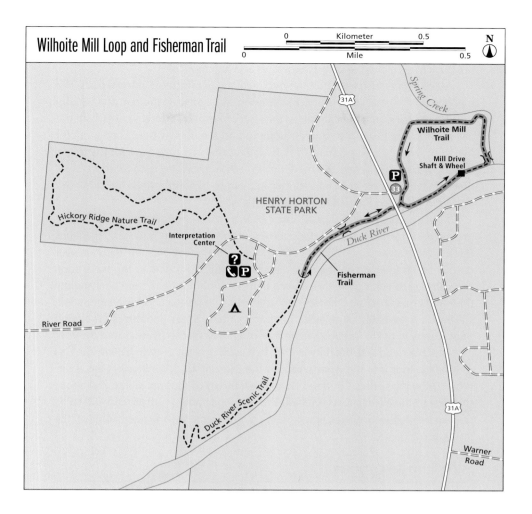

Kilometer
0   0.5
0   Mile   0.5

N

31A

Spring Creek

Wilhoite Mill
Trail

Mill Drive
Shaft & Wheel

P
33

HENRY HORTON
STATE PARK

Hickory Ridge Nature Trail

Interpretation
Center

?
P

Duck River

Fisherman
Trail

River Road

Duck River Scenic Trail

31A

Warner
Road

River is on the right, as is the US 31A bridge over the river. Pass some more remnants of the mill and a short path leading down to the river. A few flat limestone outcrops cross the trail. The river is about 15 feet below the trail and about 75 feet wide. In the spring damselflies can be seen as they hatch from the water.

Follow the trail as it takes a hard left away from the river, heading northwest into the woods. Local legend claims there is a haunted spring in the area. Cross a wood bridge, bear left, and within 50 feet cross two short sections of boardwalk over gullies. Bear right at the end of the boardwalks, heading southeast. Spring Creek can be seen to the right as it heads for the river, while the trail weaves back and forth through the trees. In the spring watch for butterflies, including white and yellow sulphurs, painted ladies, and least skippers. High bluffs can be seen across the Duck River, along the limestone ledges and outcrops.

Make a hard left away from the river, heading south through the woods. The trail generally heads south but constantly zigzags between the oak and hickory trees. In the fall watch for squirrels as they busy themselves burying nuts from the oak and hickory trees. The squirrels hope to find the nuts as they need them for food, but often the nuts remained buried and grow into new trees for the forest. Watch for birds, including the medium-size eastern towhee, with its short beak, rust-colored sides, and black head, tail, and wings. Its song sounds like drink tea. Continue following the trail to the trailhead.

After reaching the trailhead, cross over to the sign pointing to the campground and start the out-and-back portion of the Fisherman Trail along the Duck River. Go southwest, under the US 31A bridge over the river. Bear left, with the river on the left and woods on the right. Limestone outcrops come to the trail's edge and can be seen along the river. Pass a bench on the right and then bear slightly right and cross a bridge. Immediately cross another bridge and bear slightly left, still heading generally southwest. The river is within 15 feet, and this offers a good opportunity to get to its edge, where fishermen may be seen throughout the year.

Reach a Y and take the right branch as it leads up a set of steps. Follow the trail as it bears right into the woods, toward the campground. Wildflowers are abundant during the spring. Continue along the trail, which runs parallel to and above the river, to three steel posts across it. This is a good spot to turn around and backtrack to the trailhead, while enjoying and possibly exploring the river's edge on the return trip.

MILES AND DIRECTIONS

0.0 Start at the Wilhoite Mill Loop Trail trailhead adjoining the south side of the parking area.

0.1 Follow the dirt trail slightly down and toward the Duck River. In less than 0.1 mile, pass the remains of the mill and dam. Continue along the river's edge.

0.2 Pass the trailhead for the Fisherman Trail on the left. Continue following the trail northeast along the river.

0.4 Reach a wood bridge over a gully. Cross the bridge and bear left, proceeding about 50 feet to boardwalks over shallow gullies. Bear right at the end of the boardwalks.

0.6 Pass under some power lines with utility posts on the right. Follow the trail as it tracks right and left through the woods. Bear left (north) away from the river and follow Spring Creek on the right.

0.8 Reach a wood bench facing Spring Creek. At the end of the bench, bear hard left, still following along the creek edge. The creek may be dry during the summer.

0.9 Bear left away from the creek and head generally south, back toward the trailhead.

1.0 Reach the Wilhoite Mill Loop trailhead and continue the hike by taking the Fisherman Trail. A sign points toward the campground. Go under the US 31A bridge over the Duck River, which is on the left.

1.3 Reach a wood bridge and cross it, bearing slightly right at the end. Immediately cross another bridge and bear slightly left. The Duck River is on the left, about 15 feet away. At the Y; take the right branch as it heads up a set of steps (the left branch dead-ends). Follow the trail southwest along the river's edge.

1.4 Reach three steel posts across the trail. Turn around and backtrack to the trailhead.

1.9 End the hike at the trailhead.

This hike is for those who appreciate history, archeology, rivers, and waterfalls. You will visit the remains of a Native American ceremonial mound. Pass the remains of an old paper mill, and investigate two waterfalls Wildflowers are especially abundant during the spring. The mix of the Duck River and woods creates ideal habitat for many species of birds and animals.

Start: Trailhead at the rear of the museum
Distance: 2.2-mile clockwise loop
Approximate hiking time: 1.5 hours
Difficulty: Moderate due to steep slopes and narrow trail
Trail surface: Dirt, wood mulch, rock
Best season: Year-round
Other trail users: Dog walkers
Canine compatibility: Leashed dogs permitted
Fees and permits: None required
Schedule: 8:00 a.m. to sunset

Maps: USGS: Manchester; trail maps and brochures available at museum/visitor center
Trail contact: Old Stone Fort State Archaeological Park, 732 Old Stone Fort Dr., Manchester, TN 37355; (931) 723-5073; www.state .tn/environment/parks
Other: Water fountains and restrooms are available at the museum/visitor center. There is no potable water or restrooms on the trail. Take adequate water, use insect repellant and sunscreen, and wear a hat and sturdy shoes.

Finding the trailhead: From the east side of Nashville, take I-40 East via the ramp on the left toward Knoxville and go 4 miles. Keep right to take I-24 East via exit 213A toward Chattanooga and go 58.8 miles. Take TN 53, exit 110, toward Manchester and go 0.2 mile. Keep right at the fork to get on TN 53 and go 0.9 mile. Turn left onto Murfreesboro Highway and go 0.5 mile to Manchester and the entrance to Old Stone Fort. Follow the park road until it ends at the parking area by the museum/visitor center and trailhead. *DeLorme Tennessee Atlas & Gazetteer:* Page 22, A4. GPS: N35 29.23' / W86 06.09'

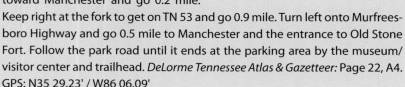

THE HIKE

The Mounds Loop, which is what I call a combination of several trails, is in Old Stone Fort Park, a Tennessee archaeological site, in Manchester. The 2.2-mile triangular-shaped trail goes in a clockwise direction around and up and down the perimeter of the fifty-acre site, which was originally enclosed by the mounds. The Duck River parallels the northern portion of the hike, while the Little Duck borders the southeast edge. Archeologists have come to the conclusion that this site was constructed by Native Americans and used for ceremonial purposes. The mounds date back 2,000 years and are believed to have been used for 500 years. Tennessee's first white settlers noticed the mounds and assumed they were the remains of an abandoned fort, hence the park's name.

Stop at the visitor center/museum before your hike and pick up a map and interpretive guide. Leave the museum, follow the sidewalk, and take the stairs on the right, leading to an observation area and the trailhead. Watch your step, and keep young children in hand, as there are roots and rocks that can be tripped over and the trail skirts the edge of 80-foot-high cliffs. Follow the trail, bearing right, into the entrance of the mounds enclosure. Head slightly down, heading southwest, and look for low mounds on the left. At about 0.2 mile pass a sign that says the wall

The Big Falls of the Duck River is located along the Mounds Trail.

turns to meet the cliffs here. The trail weaves through the woods, and very large tree roots cross the trail.

Reach a Y and take the left branch that leads sharply down to the Little Duck River. Explore the river's edge and backtrack a short distance up the hill. Continue about 30 feet and reach a marker showing the Yellow Trail to the left and the Red and Green Trails to the right. Follow the Green Trail to the right, still heading generally southwest. Bear right and in a short distance reach a Y and a sign on the left reading Forks of the River and Backbone and Little Duck River Loop. Turn left onto the Forks of the River Trail, heading generally south, and reach the confluence of the Duck and Little Duck Rivers. Watch for deer, especially in the early morning or late afternoon.

Come to a T and take the left branch, which is the Yellow, Red, and Green Trails. The right branch is the Blue Trail. Limestone outcrops across the trail serve as steps. The Duck River used to flow through the valley to the left. The valley, which is called the Moat, is really the abandoned riverbed.

At about 1.5 miles reach a Y; take the left branch onto the Old Stone Fort Loop Trail. Notice the 3-foot-high earth wall on the right. The left edge of the trail drops off about 100 feet. Follow the trail as it bears hard right, heading northeast toward the Big Falls of the Duck River. Fire pinks and wild columbines grow along the rocks. Some sections of the trail are steep and strenuous, so use caution. Continue heading generally east, and after 1,000 feet the Big Falls can be seen on the left. Come to a Y and take the left branch, then immediately reach another Y and take the left branch, heading down this steep slope toward the falls. The falls are about 40 feet high and wide, and are very picturesque and photo worthy. This is a good spot to find a rock to sit on and contemplate your surroundings. The "wall" (mounds) of the Old Stone Fort begins above the falls and continues east to the entrance. Explore the falls and then follow the trail east along the river. Much of the trail surface is solid limestone.

Go up the hill on the right, creating a shortcut to reach the Old Stone Fort Loop Trail, and continue east. Pass the site of the Hickerson and Wooten Paper Company, which flourished in the 1870s, then continue east and reach Blue Hole Falls, below the trail on the left. Head down, taking a short out and back to the falls. Return to the Old Fort Loop Trail and reach the T where the loop started, then backtrack the short distance to the trailhead.

Native Americans made arrow shafts from arrowwood, a thin-stemmed shrub.

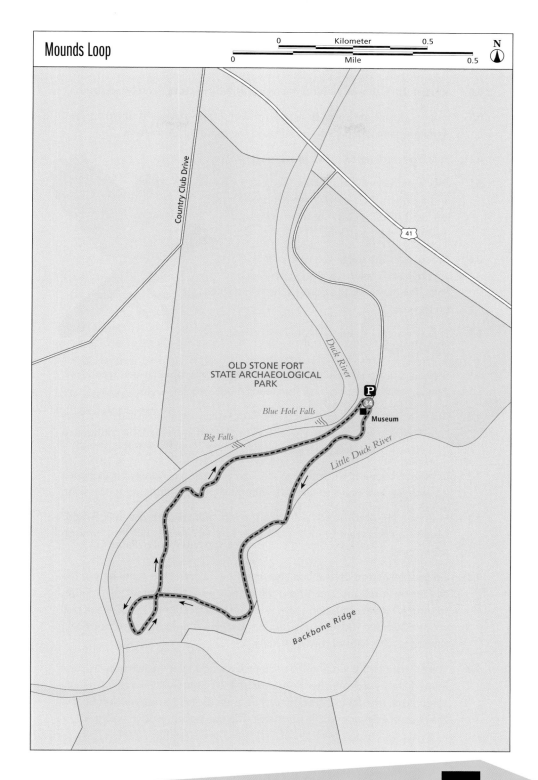

Mounds Loop

0 — Kilometer — 0.5
0 — Mile — 0.5

N

Country Club Drive

41

Duck River

OLD STONE FORT
STATE ARCHAEOLOGICAL
PARK

Blue Hole Falls

Big Falls

P

34

Museum

Little Duck River

Backbone Ridge

MILES AND DIRECTIONS

0.0 Start at the trailhead behind the museum/visitor center and head south.

0.1 Before 0.1 mile, pass a path on the right and take a hard left down a slope. A maintenance road is on the left, and the mounds are in view.

0.2 Reach a Y. and take the left branch.

0.5 Pass a path on the right that leads to a clearing and a bench. There is a sharp drop-off to the left as the trail heads slightly down and meanders right and left.

0.6 Reach a Y and take the left branch, which leads down to the Little Duck River. Follow along the edge of the river, which is on the left.

0.8 Follow the trail, bearing slightly left, as you pass the Wall Trail.

0.9 Reach a small marker at a Y. Take the right branch, which is the Green Trail. Pass a marker pointing back that reads ABANDONED RIVER OR MOAT TRAIL.

1.0 Reach a sign that reads FORKS OF THE RIVER AND BACKBONE and LITTLE DUCK RIVER LOOP. Follow the Forks of the River Trail on the left and reach the confluence of the Duck and Little Duck Rivers.

1.2 Continue following the trail along the river, heading generally north. Reach a T with the Red Trail and take the left branch. The mounds are to the right.

1.3 In about 150 yards reach a T; take the left branch onto the Yellow/Red/ Green Trail. The right branch is the Blue Trail. Follow this dirt trail through the woods.

1.5 Go up a few steps on the trail and reach a Y. Take the left branch onto the Old Stone Fort Loop Trail (the right branch leads to a meadow). A 3-foot mound is to the right, and there is a bench here. The left edge of the trail drops off about 100 feet; use caution. Bear hard right, heading northeast toward the Big Falls of the Duck River.

1.7 The falls are to the left and below. Reach a Y and take the left branch, then immediately reach another Y and take the left branch. Follow down a fairly steep slope with limestone outcrops to reach the falls, using caution. Follow the river, heading generally northeast. The trail becomes solid limestone.

1.8 Go up the hill on the right to reach the Old Stone Fort Loop Trail. After reaching the trail, follow it to the left. In less than 100 yards, reach a Y and take the right branch. The "wall" (mound) will be on the left and only 2 to 3 feet high.

2.0 Follow the trail as it weaves through the trees and reach an old paper mill site. Some stones and pieces of iron machinery remain. Follow the trail a short distance until reaching a Y; take the right branch, which tracks above the wall. The left branch heads down below the wall. Pass Blue Hole Falls down the hill and to the left.

2.1 Follow the trail down several steps, then make a hard right and reach a T. Take the left branch and backtrack the short distance to the trailhead and museum/visitor center.

2.2 End the hike at the trailhead.

A board along the trail marks a small mound, part of the original mounds surrounding the Old Fort site.

Clarksville Greenway: Zone C

People who enjoy jogging, biking, pushing a stroller, or walking their dog on a paved trail will like this hike. The shaded trail passes by limestone outcrops and boulders, some of which have taken on different colors instead of the usual gray. Watch for birds flying across the trail.

Start: Greenway Trail trailhead for Zone C. adjacent to the paved parking area
Distance: 1.5 miles out and back.
Approximate hiking time: 1 hour
Difficulty: Easy due to flat paved trail
Trail surface: Asphalt
Best season: Year-round
Other trail users: Joggers, bicyclists, skateboarders, strollers, wheelchairs, dog walkers
Canine compatibility: Leashed dogs permitted

Fees and permits: None required
Schedule: Dawn to dusk
Maps: USGS: Clarksville
Trail contact: Clarksville Parks and Recreation Department, 104 Public Square, Clarksville, TN 37040; (931) 645-7476; www.cityofclarksville.tn.us
Other: A porta-potty is located at the edge of the parking area. There is no potable water or restrooms on the trail. Take adequate water, use insect repellant and sunscreen, and wear a hat.

Finding the trailhead: From the north side of Nashville, take I-40 West toward Memphis and go 0.8 mile. Merge onto I-65 North via exit 208 toward I-24 West and go 2.1 miles. Merge onto I-24 West via exit 86A on the left and go 2.2 miles. Keep left to 1-24 West via exit 88B toward Clarksville and go 40 miles. Take US-79 South, exit 4 toward Clarksville for 0.5 mile, to TN 374N, and continue 5.2 miles to Peachers Mill Road and turn left onto Peachers Road and go 1.0 mile. Turn left onto Carter Road and go 0.3 mile, then turn right onto Helton Drive for 0.4 mile. Turn left onto Pollard Rd. and proceed 1.5 mile to 1101 Pollard Rd. *DeLorme Tennessee Atlas & Gazetteer:* Page 64, D1. GPS: N36 34.295' W87 226'

THE HIKE

This 1.5-mile out-and-back hike is a section of the Clarksville Greenway system. This section, called Zone C, is located at the east end of Pollard Road. Even though the greenway is bordered by fences on either side, its location on the top of a ridge and mostly in woods gives the appearance of a much larger area. Unusual limestone outcrops along the trail's edge also add interest. A fork of the Red River passes nearby, on the northeast, but cannot be seen. Stay on the right side of the trail to give other users the opportunity to pass, and always give notice when passing people (on the left) using strollers or wheelchairs. This is a busy trail, so stay alert to others.

A hiker investigates limestone containing embedded shells and fossils.

Begin your hike at the Greenway Trail trailhead adjacent to the large paved parking area and head north. The asphalt trail is on the top of a ridge, and both sides are lined with an intermittent three-wire rope fence to mark the greenway boundaries. The fence also protects from the sometimes steep slope down to the valley floor. Two feet of mowed grass creates a buffer from the trail's edge to the fence. Benches and a few picnic tables are conveniently placed along the trail, which is bordered by hardwood trees, including oak, hickory, and maple, on each side. The maples are easily recognized during the fall by their colorful display of red leaves. Look for vines climbing up the tree trunks, including wild grape. Pass a picnic table on the left and follow the asphalt trail as it starts to bend northwest.

Birds are easy to see and hear, especially during the spring. Watch and listen for the yellow-throated vireo. This small bird, just a little longer than the width of an adult's hand, can be recognized by its song, a repetition of a low-pitched, two- or three-note phrase of three *eights,* separated by long pauses. Its most noticeable features are its bright yellow "spectacles," yellow breast, and white wing bars on olive to gray wings. This bird can easily be confused with the pine warbler. Also watch for mockingbirds, the state bird of both Tennessee and Texas. These are medium-size birds, about the width of two hands, and can be recognized by their silvery gray head and back, and light gray chest. White wing patches may be seen when they fly. The mockingbird cannot readily be recognized by its song because it can imitate at least forty different sounds. It is a very animated bird but sometimes can be seen sitting on the tops of bushes. This is a fun bird to watch. Try making sounds to see if one will try to copy them. Take along a bird guide to add an extra dimension to the hike.

Keep bearing slightly left as the trail heads west. Pass some mounds and large limestone outcrops that border the trail's edge. The limestone, sometimes forming a short wall and other times standing 20 feet high, seems out of place here. Some pieces have a hint of orange coloring instead of the normal slate gray, while others have small pieces of rock and fossils imbedded in their surface. Several small sinkholes reach nearly to the trail's edge. The limestone and sinkholes indicate this area is on the fringe of a karst. This is a very interesting section and the high point of the hike. With the limestone as a backdrop, good photo opportunities present themselves. After investigating the limestone, continue following the trail west.

> 🌱 **Green Tip:**
> *When hiking in a group, walk single file on established trails*
> *to avoid widening them. If you come upon a sensitive area,*
> *spread out so you don't cut one path through the landscape.*
> *Don't create new trails where there were none before.*

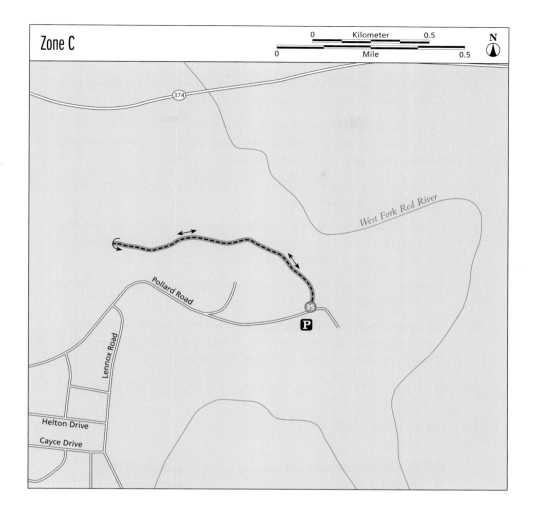

Butterflies seem to be attracted to the limestone. This may be due to the fact that some of the rock blocks have indentations that can hold water. In the spring watch for eastern black swallowtails, a large butterfly with a 3-inch wingspan. Their wings are black with two rows of cream-colored spots at the rear of each wing. They have a rapid flight, but drift when feeding on thistles and milkweed. In the afternoon watch for them perched on low shrubs. Other butterflies that may be seen include skippers and sulphurs. Continue west until reaching the end of the trail, marked by a sign, then turn around and backtrack to the trailhead.

MILES AND DIRECTIONS

0.0   Start at the Greenway Trail trailhead for the Zone C trailhead adjacent to the paved parking area and head north into the woods.

0.1   Follow the wide asphalt trail north for about 100 yards and then bend left, heading northwest. Continue straight for another 100 yards, heading northwest, and pass a picnic table on a concrete slab.

0.2   Follow the trail as it bears west. Pass a metal park bench on a concrete slab on the left and continue west.

0.3   Pass some large limestone rock formations on both the right and left while following the trail as it continues west. A hill is parallel to the left side of the trail, and the right side drops off to a valley.

0.5   Continue west while passing fencing on both the right and left sides of the trail, marking private property boundaries.

0.6   Continue west and pass a dog waste station, used for depositing plastic bags of dog waste. The limestone outcrops on the left almost form a wall. Follow the asphalt trail west as it slopes slightly up.

0.75 Reach a barricade that marks the end of the trail, then turn around and backtrack to the trailhead.

1.5   End the hike at the trailhead.

Outcroppings of limestone along the trail have embedded rocks—unusual in these outcrops.

Dunbar Cave State Natural Area: Lake Trail and Recovery Trail

36

This is a great hike for those who love nostalgia, woods, and lakes. The trail takes you up and down through the woods and around twenty-acre Swan Lake. Near the mouth of Dunbar Cave, go up the stairs to a concrete dance floor that in the late 1940s was filled with people dancing to the music of famous bands, including Tommy Dorsey's and Benny Goodman's.

Start: Recovery Trail trailhead at the edge of the visitor center parking area
Distance: 2.4-mile clockwise loop
Approximate hiking time: 1.5 hours
Difficulty: Moderate due to narrow trail and some up and down
Trail surface: Asphalt, dirt, mulch, concrete
Best season: September to June
Other trail users: Dog walkers, joggers
Canine compatibility: Leashed dogs permitted
Fees and permits: None required

Schedule: 8:00 a.m. to sunset
Maps: USGS: Clarksville; trail maps available at visitor center; large map boards along trail
Trail contact: Dunbar Cave State Natural Area, 401 Old Dunbar Rd., Clarksville, TN 37043; (931) 648-5526; www.tnstateparks.com
Other: Water fountains and restrooms are available at the visitor center. There is no potable water or restrooms on the trail. Take adequate drinking water, use insect repellent and sunscreen, and wear a hat.

Finding the Trailhead: From the north side of Nashville, take I-40 West toward Memphis and go 0.8 mile. Merge onto I-65 North via exit 208 toward I-24 West and go 2.1 miles. Merge onto I-24 West via exit 86A on the left toward Clarksville and go 2.2 miles. Keep left to 1-24 West via exit 88B toward Clarksville and go 36.6 miles. Take TN 237 West, exit 8, and go 0.4 mile. Turn onto TN 237 and go 0.8 mile, then turn left onto Dunbar Cave Road and go 3 miles. Turn right onto Old Dunbar Cave Road and go 0.1 mile to 401 Old Dunbar Cave Rd. in Clarksville, then turn onto the park road and follow it to the visitor center and trailhead. *DeLorme Tennessee Atlas & Gazetteer:* Page 64, D1. GPS: N36 33.02' / W87 18.367'

THE HIKE

This 2.4-mile clockwise loop, combining the Recovery Trail and sections of Lake Trail, is located in the 110-acre Dunbar Cave State Natural Area. The entrance to Dunbar Cave was inhabited by prehistoric peoples for thousands of years before settlers arrived. They painted drawings on the cave walls, perhaps as part of religious ceremonies. This is an area of karst topography, highlighted by limestone outcrops, caves, and sinkholes. Local lore has it that the cave was a favorite location for moonshiners during the 1920s. Numerous social events, including dances, concerts, and fairs, were held around the cave.

Roy Acuff, an icon in country music and an entrepreneur, purchased Dunbar Cave in the latter half of the 1940s. He used the site for entertainment shows featuring big bands like Benny Goodman's and Tommy Dorsey's. Big bands and dancing were the rage in the 1940s, and it was during this period that a large concrete structure, with three distinct arches, was poured in front of the cave entrance to serve as a dance floor and concession area. This striking structure is intact today, with the cave behind it and Swan Lake in front of it. Over time the popularity of the cave and surrounding area declined, and Acuff sold the property to the state.

The concrete dance floor and concession area in front of Dunbar Cave were very popular in the 1940s.

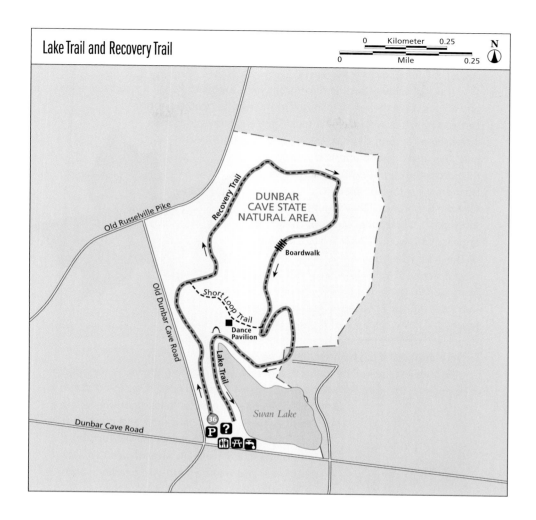

Begin your hike at the Recovery Trail trailhead, which is adjacent to the visitor center parking area. Swan Lake is on the right, and several purple martin houses are scattered about the grounds around the parking area. Just before reaching the woods, pass several picnic tables on the right and left, then go up a slope, heading north, into the mature hardwoods. Large beech trees, 3 feet in diameter, are within 6 feet of the trail. They can be identified by their smooth gray bark, and they retain their crumpled leaves during the winter. The trail is wide and surfaced with crushed gravel. Large batches of poison ivy, in the form of a bush or climbing vine, are on both sides of the trail. Learn to recognize this potential hike spoiler, identified by its three leaves.

The trail weaves back and forth between the trees. Reach a small trail map and a Y and take the left branch, still in the woods, heading north. Dirt and mulch now surface the trail. There are a few cedar trees interspersed among the oak, beech, and sycamore trees, and the trees' shade furnishes welcome relief from the sun. The woods can be very humid during the summer. Reach a Y and take the left branch, following it to the right (northeast). Limestone outcrops begin to appear in the woods and reach to the edge of the trail, which has some water bars placed across it to help reduce erosion from rainfall. Those using GPS equipment may have difficulty getting reception through the heavy tree cover. Sections of the trail bear hard left and then hard right, temporarily heading in various directions for very short distances but then returning northeast.

Continue following the trail as it slopes up, until reaching the top of the ridge. A bench is on the right, furnishing a spot to rest a few minutes. In a short distance bear hard right, heading south. In less than the length of a football field, make a hard right and head west. The trail flattens and then heads down. Turn right, heading west until reaching a boardwalk. Cross the boardwalk and make a hard left, heading south. Woods still surround both sides of the trail. Follow the trail up and down small slopes for less than 0.5 mile until reaching a T. Take the left branch, staying on the Recovery Trail and heading west. Continue following the trail until making a hard right as the trail doubles back on itself, then after a short distance cross a bridge over a gully. Start to bear right, heading north and then northwest, as the trail approaches Swan Lake.

Reach the edge of the lake, where there is a bench facing the water. Turn right at the bench onto the Lake Trail and head north. Continue following the trail along the water's edge and notice the many ducks that frequent the lake year-round. The large white concrete structure that used to house the dance floor is straight ahead. Go up the steps to explore the building, then return to the trail and follow it back to the visitor center and trailhead.

0.0   Start at the Recovery Trail trailhead adjacent to the visitor center parking area and head north.

0.1   Pass picnic tables on the right and left. Woods are on both sides of the trail as it slopes up and down. Swan Lake is on the right but usually not visible.

0.2   Bear right, pass a guardrail, and reach a trail map and Y. Take the left branch, heading north. The right branch is a short leg to Dunbar Cave. Continue following the trail north, passing over some water bars made from 6-by-6 lumber.

0.3   Reach a Y and take the left branch, which is the Recovery Trail (the right branch is a short loop back to the trailhead). Continue following the trail as it bears hard right and heads northeast.

0.5   Bear hard left, temporarily heading northwest, then bear right and pass a wood park bench on the right. Continue straight on the trail, through the hardwood trees, going northeast and slightly up. The trail flattens for a short distance, after which it weaves a bit and slopes up.

0.7   Reach the top of the ridge and make a hard right, heading east. Pass a park bench on the right. Continue bearing slightly to the right (east) as the trail slopes down. Bear hard right and follow the trail south. Continue following the trail as it makes a hard right and heads west.

1.0   Pass a park bench and make a hard left, heading south, and cross over a boardwalk. At the end of the boardwalk bear right and then left as the trail follows up and down slopes. Continue following the trail generally south, although it zigzags a little.

1.4   Follow the trail south as it undulates up and down and then has flat sections. Reach a T and take the left branch, heading east on the Recovery Trail (the left branch leads to the Short Loop Trail). Bear slightly left and then follow right, heading west.

1.7 Bear hard right, heading temporarily north as the trail doubles back on itself. The trail then bears left until it is heading west. Cross a short bridge over a gully. Start to bear right, heading north. Follow the trail down, bearing northwest through the woods as it approaches the lake.

2.0 Reach a bench at the lake's edge and turn right onto the Lake Trail, heading north. The trail borders the lake.

2.? Continue north until reaching a large white concrete structure. Go up the steps to explore the dance pavilion. Return to the Lake Trail and follow it along the edge of the lake, heading south to the visitor center.

2.4 End the hike at the visitor center.

🌿 Green Tip:
Pack out what you pack in, even food scraps because they can attract wild animals.

Nashville-Area Hiking Club

Tennessee Trails Association
P.O. Box 41446
Nashville, TN 37204
888-HIKE-TTA (888-445-3882)
www.tennesseetrails.org

Hike Index

Sidebar Index

About the Author

Keith Stelter is a columnist for the HCN newspaper group and has been hiking, writing, and taking photographs for forty years. He has hiked national park trails with his father and has hiked extensively in the Nashville area. His twin daughters were born in Nashville. Keith is a member of the Outdoor Writers Association of America, Texas Master Naturalists, North American Nature Photographers Association, and American Trails Association. He is the author of several books about Texas, including *Best Hikes Near Austin and San Antonio, Best Hikes Near Houston,* and Best Easy Day Hike guides for Austin, Houston, and San Antonio. His avocation as a naturalist allows him to add interesting and educational information to his writing. He lives in Tomball, Texas.

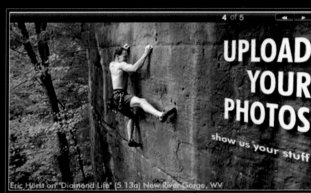